2 0

THE
MARINER'S
BOOK of DAYS

PETER H. SPECTRE

Sheridan House

A special thank-you to those who have helped in the creation of this work:
Lothar Simon, Janine Simon, Kathleen Brandes, and Lindy Gifford.
And heaps of praise for Llewellyn Howland III,
who conceived this work many years ago and encouraged its creation.

Published 2013 by
Sheridan House
Distributed by National Book Network
4501 Forbes Boulevard
Suite 200
Lanham, MD 20706

Design by Sherry Streeter and Lindy Gifford

Cover art: *Rough Return to Jonesport*
Artist: Robert Dance Website: www.robertdance.com
Courtesy of J. Russell Jinishian Gallery, Inc. Website: www.jrusselljinishiangallery.com

Printed in the United States of America

ISBN 9781574093162

For all at last return to the sea–to Oceanus, the ocean river,
like the everflowing river of time, the beginning and the end.

—Rachel Carson

The Pool from Ratcliff Stairs

In the beginning God created the heaven and the earth. And the earth was without form, and void; and darkness was upon the face of the deep. And the Spirit of God moved upon the face of the water.
—King James Bible, Genesis 1:1–2

He that will learn to pray, let him go to sea.
—George Herbert

The sea carries no tracks; one disappears into it and leaves no trace, returns from it without a mark to show whence one came.
—Edward L. Beach

It isn't that life ashore is distasteful to me. But life at sea is better.
—Sir Francis Drake

The wind is free, and we're bound for sea,
  Heave away cheerily, ho, oh!
The lasses are waving to you and me,
  As off to the South'ard we go.
—from an old anchor song

THE ANTARCTIC EXPLORATION SHIP *TERRA NOVA*, OFF CAPE CROZIER, ROSS SEA, JANUARY 3, 1911

We came up to the Barrier five miles east of the Cape soon after 1 P.M. The swell from the E.N.E. continued to the end. The Barrier was not more than 60 feet in height. From the crow's nest one could see well over it, and noted that there was a gentle slope for at least a mile towards the edge. The land of Black (or White?) Island could be seen distinctly behind, topping the huge lines of pressure ridges.… The Barrier takes a sharp turn back at 2 or 3 miles from the cliffs, runs back for half a mile, then west again with a fairly regular surface until within a few hundred yards of the cliffs; the interval is occupied with a single high pressure ridge—the evidences of pressure at the edge being less marked than I had expected. Ponting was very busy with cinematograph and camera. In the angle at the corner near the cliffs Rennick got a sounding of 140 fathoms and Nelson some temperatures and samples. When lowering the water bottle on one occasion the line suddenly became slack at 100 metres, then after a moment's pause began to run out again. We are curious to know the cause, and imagine the bottle struck a seal or whale.
—Captain Robert Falcon Scott

HOW WILL WE UNDERSTAND HISTORY IF WE FORGET THE EXPERIENCE OF SEAFARING?

The number of people able to realize how the ships of the Armada were saved from destruction on the Zealand banks by a shift of wind at the last moment, or who can grasp what Anson had to contend with, or appreciate the splendid daring of Hawke is much smaller than it was a hundred years ago, and history will deteriorate unless its tellers experience something of the difficulties and hazard that used to be taken as a matter of course.
—Alan Moore, writing in 1925

*We should all be the fitter, the happier and better if we
could return to the wide horizons of land and sea.*
                                        —Basil Lubbock

DEC/JAN

Monday
30

1915—The Australian sailing passenger ship *Ivanhoe*,
once one of the most popular on the Britain-to-
Melbourne run, was wrecked at Honolulu, Hawaii.

Tuesday
31 NEW YEAR'S EVE

1923—The first transatlantic shortwave radio voice
message was transmitted from Pittsburgh, Pennsylvania,
to Manchester, England, and then retransmitted from
there to London.

Wednesday
1 NEW YEAR'S DAY

1861—*The Rowing Almanack*, a British journal
covering competition rowing, began publication.

Thursday
2

1889—The Maryland state steamer *Helen Baughman*,
enforcing Chesapeake Bay oyster-dredging laws,
fought a pitched battle with the unlicensed dredging
schooner *Robert McAllister*.

Friday
3

1942—Five Sullivan brothers—George Thomas,
Francis Henry, Joseph Eugene, Madison Abel, and
Albert Leo—enlisted in the U.S. Navy; all were lost
the following November when the cruiser *Juneau*
was sunk in battle off Guadalcanal.

Saturday ○
4

1910—The first U.S. battleship of the dreadnought
type, USS *Michigan*, was commissioned.

Sunday
5

1818—The Black Ball Line commenced regularly
scheduled transatlantic packet service, the first of its
kind, between Liverpool, England, and New York City.

THE THREE-MASTED TOPSAIL-YARD SCHOONER *SUNBEAM* AT THE INTERNATIONAL DATE LINE, PACIFIC OCEAN, JANUARY 12, 1877

Today the order of things is reversed, and we are now twelve hours behind our friends at home. Having quitted one side of the map of the world (according to Mercator's projection), and entered upon the other half, we begin to feel that we are at last really "homeward bound." At four a.m. Powell [the engineer] woke us with the announcement that the boiler-tube had again burst, and that we had consequently ceased steaming. Letting off steam, and blowing out the boiler, made a tremendous noise, which aroused everybody in the ship. It was a lovely morning, but a flat calm, and the sun rose magnificently. The few light clouds near the surface of the water caught and reflected the rays of light most brilliantly before the sun itself appeared, and assumed all manner of fanciful shapes.

            —Lady Annie Brassey

JACQUES-YVES COUSTEAU

Jacques-Yves Cousteau (1910–1997), a French naval officer, first gained fame as the co-inventor of the aqualung, aka SCUBA (Self-Contained Underwater Breathing Apparatus). Following that with the development of improved techniques for underwater photography, cinematography, and, later, video, he became a spokesman for the protection of the ocean environment. He and his crew roamed the oceans of the world in his specially equipped exploration vessel *Calypso*, producing films that won him three Oscars and served as the basis for countless television specials and the acclaimed series *The Undersea World of Jacques Cousteau*. In the meantime, he founded the Office of Underseas Research, now known as the Centre of Advanced Marine Studies, in Marseille, France; served as director of the Oceanographic Museum, Monaco; and established the Cousteau Foundation, whose mission is to foster marine research.

THE SEA IS FEMININE

The sea is like a woman: she lures us, and we run madly after her; she ill-uses us, and we adore her; beautiful, capricious, tender, and terrible! There is no satiety in this love; there never is satiety in true affection. The sea is the first thing which meets my eyes in the morning, placidly sunning herself under my window; her many voices beckoning me, her gently heaving breast alluring me, her face beaming with unutterable delight. All through the day I wanton with her; and the last thing at night, I see the long shimmering track of light from the distant beacon thrown across her tranquil surface.

            —George Henry Lewes

THE SEA IS MASCULINE

The sea has always been a seducer, a careless lying fellow, not feminine, as many writers imagine, but strongly masculine in its allurement. The king of the sea, with his whiskers of weed and his trident of dolphins, truly represents the main and gives it character. The sea, like a great sultan, supports thousands of ships, his lawful wives. These he caresses and chastises as the case may be. This explains the feminine gender of all proper vessels.

            —Felix Riesenberg

Monday
6

1838—Samuel F. B. Morse publicly demonstrated his newly developed telegraph machine for the first time.

Tuesday
7

1890—The cruiser *Baltimore*, the first ship in the U.S. Navy to be converted for minelaying (in 1915), was commissioned at Philadelphia.

Wednesday
8

1968—The first undersea television special produced by Jacques-Yves Cousteau, underwater documentarian and co-inventor of the aqualung, was aired.

Thursday
9

1952—The steamship *Pennsylvania*, with a tremendous sea running, developed a 14-foot crack in the port side of her hull and sank in the Pacific Ocean west of Cape Flattery, Washington; all 45 men in her crew were lost.

Friday
10

1834—The New York Amateur Boat Club Association, Castle Garden, the first affiliation of boating clubs in the United States, was organized in New York.

Saturday
11

1875—The Nautical School of the Port of New York, the first maritime academy in the United States, opened aboard the full-rigged sailing ship *St. Mary*, New York City.

Sunday
12

1920—The French passenger ship *L'Afrique* sank in the Bay of Biscay; 553 lives were lost.

PERSONAL GEAR REQUIRED FOR ENLISTED MEN, U.S. NAVY, LATE 19TH CENTURY

    2 caps
    3 cap covers
    1 black silk neck handkerchief
    3 blue flannel overshirts
    3 undershirts
    3 drawers—if worn
    1 pair blue cloth pants
    2 pairs satinet pants
    3 white frocks
    3 pairs white pants
    2 pairs socks
    2 pairs shoes
    1 flannel jumper
    1 white jumper
    badges as per regulation
    1 white straw hat

THE MID-NINETEENTH-CENTURY MERCHANT SAILOR'S GARB, ACCORDING TO RICHARD HENRY DANA, JR.

A sailor has a peculiar cut to his clothes, and a way of wearing them which a green hand can never get. The trousers, tight around the hips, and thence hanging long and loose round the feet, a superabundance of checked shirt, a low-crowned, well-varnished black hat, worn on the back of the head, with half a fathom of black ribbon hanging over the left eye, and a slip-tie to the black silk neckerchief, with sundry other minutiae, are signs, the want of which betrays the beginner at once.

OILSKINS, AKA "OILEYS"

Oilskins were made with unbleached white cotton cloth. After the garment was made—pants, jacket, long coat, hat, or apron—it was made waterproof as follows:

$1/2$ pound shredded paraffin wax was dissolved in one gallon of warm kerosene in a large pot.

The garment was dipped in the mixture and excess fluid was squeezed out, then it was hung to dry either outdoors or in a well-ventilated space.

When dry, two thin coats of a mixture of 1 part kerosene and 1 part varnish was brushed on, with special attention paid to the seams.

Light-yellow oilskins were made with light-colored oil; black oilskins were coated with a blackish oil.

THE U.S. BATTLESHIP *KANSAS*, GUANTANAMO BAY, CUBA, JANUARY 15, 1912

The "Lucky Bag," and then began the fun. For weeks the watchful eye of the Master-at-Arms, the ship's chief-of-police, had been at work seeking "articles adrift," as he called them, and now all the contents were to be sold at auction to the highest bidder. For extreme tidiness is a pronounced characteristic in Uncle Sam's Navy. "A place for everything and everything in its place," is the way they put it, and woe to the forgetful or careless bluejacket who leaves anything belonging to him where it ought not to be. Into the lucky bag it goes, and to redeem it the culprit must either acknowledge his ownership at once and incur a light fine for his offense, or else await the quarterly sale and then hope to be able to bid high enough to get his own once more. It is a time-honored institution, as old as the navy itself, and indeed one of the most effective ways ever devised of maintaining that state of order which has come to be a by-word in the service.

—Robert W. Neeser

Monday ◑
13

1853—The ship *Cornelius Grinnell* went aground in a heavy surf off Squan Beach, New Jersey; all 234 persons on board were rescued by lifecar, a lifeboat specially designed for work in surf.

Tuesday
14

1996—More than 50 hockey gloves—lost when several shipping containers went overboard from a Pacific freighter—washed ashore on Vancouver Island, British Columbia.

Wednesday
15

1836—The Secretary of the Treasury prescribed that henceforth blue instead of the previous gray would be the color of dress uniforms of officers in the Revenue Cutter Service, forerunner of the U.S. Coast Guard.

Thursday
16

1891—The speedster *Scud* of the Shrewsbury Ice Yacht Club won a 20-mile race for the ice-yacht championship of America.

Friday
17

1929—Popeye, the archetypal sailorman, appeared for the first time in the comic strip *Thimble Theatre*, by Elzie Segar.

Saturday
18

1926—The four-masted Nova Scotia schooner *W.H. Eastwood*, a rumrunner waiting to unload on "Rum Row" off Long Island, New York, came under fire from a U.S. Coast Guard cutter.

Sunday
19

1996—Captain Grover Sanschagrin, a docking pilot in the port of New York, docked the 40,000th ship of his career, a record to date.

USE OF OIL IN CALMING THE SEA

In using oil for this purpose, the one great difficulty is to have the oil reach the water far enough to windward to give the ship the benefit of its effect. This may be effected by attaching an oil bag to a drag, in case the ship is hove-to with that contrivance.

Running before the wind, oil bags should be towed from both catheads. The tow-line should be of such length as may be necessary to keep the bags in the water.

Hove-to with or without a drag, an oil bag on the weather bow, one about midships and one on the quarter will have a modifying effect.

Mineral oils are of little or no use for this purpose. Animal or vegetable oils are satisfactory. In cold weather, the effect of oil on rough water is considerably less than in warm weather, for the simple reason that the oil thickens and will not spread freely. The result of experiments covering a period of several years seems to indicate that lard oil gives the most satisfactory results.

Oil bags should be made of canvas, and of sufficient size to hold oakum enough to absorb from one to two gallons of oil, and there should be holes in the bag of sufficient size to permit the oil to leak out, and to admit the water in quantities large enough to act as an agent in making the leakage uniform.

Many navigators have condemned oil bags for the simple reason that the oil could not escape; the holes being small, having been made with a sail needle. The holes should be at least one-quarter of an inch in diameter.

—from *The Navigator or Mariner's Guide*, 1905

SMALL BOATS FROM HMS *BEAGLE*, OFF TIERRA DEL FUEGO, JANUARY 20, 1833

Magnificent glaciers extend from the mountain side to the water's edge. They are covered by a wide mantle of perpetual snow, and numerous cascades pour their waters, through the woods, into the narrow channel below.... The boats being hauled on shore at our dinner-hour, we were admiring from the distance of half a mile a perpendicular cliff of ice, and were wishing that some more fragments would fall. At last, down came a mass with a roaring noise, and immediately we saw the smooth outline of a wave travelling towards us. The men ran down as quickly as they could to the boats; for the chance of their being dashed to pieces was evident. One of the seamen just caught hold of the bows, as the curling breaker reached it: he was knocked over and over, but not hurt, and the boats though thrice lifted on high and let fall again, received no damage. This was most fortunate for us, for we were a hundred miles distant from the ship, and we should have been left without provisions or fire-arms.

—Charles Darwin

"HOPE" IS THE THING WITH FEATHERS
by Emily Dickinson

"Hope" is the thing with feathers
That perches in the soul
And sings the tune without the words
And never stops at all,

And sweetest in the gale is heard;
And sore must be the storm
That could abash the little bird
That kept so many warm.

I've heard it in the chillest land
And on the strangest sea,
Yet never, in extremity,
It asked a crumb of me.

*A favorable wind with mysterious touch carries
you whithersoever you steer, as if on a path of oil.*
—William Forwell

JANUARY

Monday ●
20 MARTIN LUTHER KING DAY

1877—The steamship *George Washington* stranded
off Mistaken Point, Newfoundland; 25 lives were lost.

Tuesday
21

1877—The downeaster *Grandee* collided head-on
with an iceberg in the Southern Ocean and survived,
one of the few wooden ships to do so.

Wednesday
22

Two U.S. Navy destroyers—USS *Reno* (1919) and
USS *Bulmer* (1920)—were launched on this day.

Thursday
23

1622—William Baffin, navigator and explorer after
whom the Arctic's Baffin Island was named, died
on Kishm Island in the Persian Gulf.

Friday
24

1885—The crew of the merchant ship *Kirkwood*,
sinking in heavy weather, calmed the seas by
pouring salmon oil from the cargo over the side;
all were saved by the steamer *Barrowmore*.

Saturday
25

1964—The SS *Mormacargo*, the first American-
flagged fully automated cargo ship, requiring
a crew of only 32 instead of the usual 49, was
launched in Pascagoula, Mississippi.

Sunday
26

1884—The ice-yacht *Dreadnought* set a
frozen-water speed record by sailing 1 mile in
1 minute, 10 seconds, at Red Bank, New Jersey.

So long as I was at sea, or isolated with the Navy in its majestic activities, I was happy and serene.
—Filson Young

PRESIDENTS WHO SERVED IN THE U.S. NAVY

John F. Kennedy
Lyndon B. Johnson
Richard M. Nixon
Gerald R. Ford
James Earl "Jimmy" Carter
George H. W. Bush

THE EXPLORATION SHIP FRAM, BAY OF WHALES, ANTARCTICA, JANUARY 30, 1912

Our farewell to this snug harbour took almost the form of a leap from one world to another; the fog hung over us as thick as gruel, concealing all the surrounding outlines behind its clammy curtain, as we stood out. After a lapse of three or four hours, it lifted quite suddenly, but astern of us the bank of fog still stood like a wall; behind it the panorama, which we knew would have looked wonderful in clear weather, and which we should so gladly have let our eyes rest upon as long as we could, was entirely concealed.... When the fog lifted, we found ourselves surrounded by open sea, practically free from ice, on all sides. A blue-black sea, with a heavy, dark sky above it, is not usually reckoned among the sights that delight the eye. To our organs of vision it was a real relief to come into surroundings where dark colours predominated. For months we had been staring at a dazzling sea of white, where artificial means had constantly to be employed to protect the eyes against the excessive flood of light.

—Roald Amundsen

FAMOUS PEOPLE WHO SERVED IN THE U.S. NAVY

Jack Benny	Jackie Cooper
Humphrey Bogart	Glenn Ford
Ernest Borgnine	Popeye
Raymond Burr	Edward Steichen
Johnny Carson	Montell Williams
Bill Cosby	Don Rickles
Henry Fonda	Jack Lemmon
Eddie Albert	Kirk Douglas
Donald Rumsfeld	Tony Curtis
MC Hammer	Yogi Berra

FAMOUS PEOPLE WHO SERVED IN THE U.S. COAST GUARD

Arnold Palmer	Buddy Ebsen
Alex Haley	Sid Caesar
Walter Cronkite	Victor Mature
Jeff Bridges	Sam Nunn
Beau Bridges	Edwin O'Connor
Fred Brooks	Claiborne Pell
Jack Dempsey	Mel Torme
Arthur Fiedler	Rudy Vallee
Arthur Godfrey	Tom Waits
Otto Graham	Thornton Wilder
Ted Turner	Gig Young

Scientiae cedit mare (The sea yields to knowledge)
—U.S. Coast Guard Academy motto

Ex scientia tridens (From knowledge, sea power)
—U.S. Naval Academy motto

Monday
27

1926—Following a four-day struggle, the crew of the U.S. freighter *President Roosevelt*, directed by Captain Robert B. Miller, saved the entire crew of the sinking British freighter *Antinoe*.

Tuesday
28

1969—Union Oil Company's Well A-21, in the Pacific Ocean off Santa Barbara, California, burst and leaked crude oil for 11 days, fouling the beaches along 200 miles of coastline.

Wednesday
29

1942—The convoy escort *Alexander Hamilton* was torpedoed by a German submarine in the Atlantic Ocean, the first U.S. Coast Guard cutter sunk by enemy action during World War II.

Thursday
30

1882—Franklin Delano Roosevelt, Assistant Secretary of the Navy under Woodrow Wilson and thirty-second president of the United States, was born in Hyde Park, New York.

Friday
31

1961—Samuel Lee Gravely Jr., the first African American to command a combat ship in the U.S. Navy, assumed command of the destroyer escort USS *Falgout*.

Saturday
1

1930—The *City of New York*, the first passenger ship to be powered by a diesel engine, got underway on its first voyage, from New York to Cape Town, South Africa.

Sunday
2

GROUNDHOG DAY
Can spring be far away?

BUYS BALLOT'S LAW

Because of the rotation of the earth, the atmospheric circulation tends to be counter-clockwise around areas of low pressure and clockwise around areas of high pressure in the Northern Hemisphere; the opposite in the Southern Hemisphere.

If an observer in the Northern Hemisphere faces the surface wind, the center of low pressure is toward his right, somewhat behind him; and the center of high pressure is toward his left and somewhat in front of him.

If an observer in the Southern Hemisphere faces the surface wind, the center of low pressure is toward his left and somewhat behind him; and the center of high pressure is toward his right and somewhat in front of him.

BAROMETRIC RULES OF THUMB

In the middle latitudes, 30.50 inches of barometric pressure at sea level is considered high, 29.50 considered low.

Persistent decrease in barometric pressure foretells foul weather.

Sudden fall in barometric pressure (over .04 inch per hour) foretells heavy winds.

Steady barometric pressure indicates fair weather.

A slow, persistent increase in barometric pressure, especially when accompanied by rising temperatures, foretells a stabilization in the weather.

A rapid rise in barometric pressure foretells unsettled weather.

A distant storm is indicated by a local drop in barometric pressure while local weather remains unchanged.

WHEN USING A BAROMETER

Pay no attention to the labels—"Fair," "Stormy," "Change," etc.—as they are generally meaningless. What's important is whether atmospheric pressure has been rising or falling.

WAITING FOR SUPPLIES AND MAIL, THE ISLAND OF TRISTAN DA CUNHA, SOUTH ATLANTIC OCEAN, FEBRUARY 4, 1905

There was a cry of "Sail, ho!" and on going out to look we saw a ship opposite the settlement. As we sat on the cliff, Mr. Bob Green suddenly jumped up crying, "Sail, ho!" and on looking, sure enough we saw a second sail coming up.... We heard a distant whistle which we knew meant the boats were coming. We thought we would go down to see them land, but as it was very dark and we had lent our lantern we had to wait till we saw a light passing our way. Most of the people were carrying brands which they waved to keep them alight, causing quite a fine effect. On the cliff a fire was burning, and another on the shore. Lanterns were held up so that the incoming boat might have all the light possible. Well as the landing-place is known, it is difficult in the darkness to steer clear of rocks and to keep the boat from filling with water in the surf. The moment it touched the shore the women, boys, and girls ran down and pulled frantically at the rope. It had to be hauled up a steep bank of shingle. The fire was stirred up and in its light the second boat made a run for the shore. It was a weird scene.

—K. M. Barrow

FEBRUARY

Monday ○
3

1894—The downeaster *Dirigo*, the first American commercial sailing vessel built of steel, was launched in Bath, Maine.

Tuesday
4

1987—The American yacht *Stars & Stripes* defeated the Australian yacht *Kookaburra III*, four races to none, to win the America's Cup.

Wednesday
5

1882—The schooner *Mary L. Vankirk* ran ashore near Chicamacomico, North Carolina, during a storm; a crew from the local lifesaving station rigged a breeches buoy and rescued all five men aboard.

Thursday
6

1808—The American sealer *Topaz*, Captain Mayhew Folger, called on Pitcairn Island in the Pacific Ocean and found there John Adams, the last surviving mutineer from HMS *Bounty*.

Friday
7

1821—John Davis, a seal hunter, stepped ashore at Hughes Bay, the first American to set foot on the continent of Antarctica.

Saturday
8

1877—Charles Wilkes, commander of the United States Exploring Expedition of 1838–42, also known as the Wilkes Expedition, died in Washington, DC.

Sunday
9

1870—The Weather Bureau was authorized by the U.S. Congress.

INTERNATIONAL DISTRESS SIGNALS, ACCORDING TO THE U.S. COAST PILOT

(1) A signal made by radiotelegraphy or by any other signaling method consisting of the group "SOS" in Morse Code.

(2) A signal sent by radiotelephony consisting of the spoken word "MAYDAY."

(3) The International Flag Code Signal of NC.

(4) A signal consisting of a square flag having above or below it a ball or anything resembling a ball.

(5) Flames on the craft (as from a burning oil barrel, etc.).

(6) A rocket parachute flare or hand flare showing a red light.

(7) Rockets or shells throwing red stars fired one at a time at short intervals.

(8) Orange smoke, as emitted from a distress flare.

(9) Slowly and repeatedly raising and lowering arms outstretched to each side.

(10) A gun or other explosive signal fired at intervals of about 1 minute.

(11) A continuous sounding of any fog-signal apparatus.

(12) The radiotelegraph alarm signal.

(13) The radiotelephone alarm signal.

(14) Signals transmitted by emergency position-indicating radiobeacons.

(15) A piece of orange-colored canvas with either a black square and circle or other appropriate symbol (for identification from the air).

(16) A dye marker.

THE GUNBOAT *DESTROYER*, BAHIA, BRAZIL, FEBRUARY 9, 1894

Everything was funeral quietness at Bahia. The doughty [Brazilian Admiral] Goncalves I saw often, passing to and fro, always to the music of a band. A captain of my grade, and foreigner at that, don't get any music in Brazil. All else was quiet and serene. The occasional pop of a champagne cork, at the "Paris" on the hill, might have been heard, but that was all, except again the sunset gun. The rising sun had to take care of itself. The average Brazilian Naval man is an amphibious being, spending his time about equally between hotel and harbor, and is never dangerous. I was astonished at the quietness of Bahia, there was not even target practice.... There was to be torpedo practice one day. A Howell torpedo was launched, but boomerang like it returned[,] hitting the ship from which it was hurled. The only thing lacking to have made it a howling success was the dynamite, which these remarkable warriors forgot to put in.

—Joshua Slocum

BE PREPARED!

Never expect anything to go as planned.

Keep emergency gear close at hand.

Know where all spares are stowed—make a list and post it.

Maintain a "culch" box—odds-and-ends for quick repairs.

Carry gear for damage control—wooden plugs of various sizes, hose clamps, sheet lead for emergency patches, pieces of leather and inner tube, several buckets, plenty of rope and marline, duct tape, seizing wire, etc.

Make up a "panic" bag in the event you have to take to the life raft; check the contents periodically.

> *Most of us, I suppose, are a little nervous of the sea. No matter what its smiles may be, we doubt its friendship.*   —H. M. Tomlinson

FEBRUARY

Monday
10

1852–The clipper ship *Sword-Fish* defeated the clipper ship *Flying Fish* by slightly more than one week in a celebrated match race from New York around Cape Horn to San Francisco.

Tuesday
11

WHITE SHIRT DAY
And please, no T-shirts

Wednesday
12 LINCOLN'S BIRTHDAY

1943–The Liberty ship *Booker T. Washington*, commanded by Hugh Mulzac, the first African American to hold an unlimited mariner's license and the first African American to command a merchant ship, docked in London, England.

Thursday
13

1934–The Soviet steamship *Chelyuskin* was crushed by ice and sank near Kolyuchin Island in the Chukchi Sea; all 111 aboard escaped onto the ice; they were rescued approximately two months later.

Friday
14 VALENTINE'S DAY

1870–The *Glory of the Seas*, the last clipper ship built by Donald McKay, set sail from New York for San Francisco on her maiden voyage.

Saturday
15

1911–The U.S. Congress assigned Fort Trumbull, New London, Connecticut, to the Treasury Department for the use of the Revenue Cutter Service, forerunner of the U.S. Coast Guard, as its cadet training school.

Sunday
16

1957–The first ship to transport fresh orange juice in stainless-steel tanks, the SS *Tropicana*, got underway from Port Canaveral, Florida, to Whitestone, New York.

I was born in a cold spot, on coldest North Mountain, on a cold February 20.... On both sides my family were sailors; and if any Slocum should be found not seafaring, he will show at least an inclination to whittle models of boats and contemplate voyages. My father was the sort of man who, if wrecked on a desolate island, would find his way home, if he had a jackknife and could find a tree.

—Joshua Slocum,
the first man to sail around the world alone

Captain Slocum is what we may call an uncommon man. —Thomas Fleming Day

THE NATURE OF THE SINGLEHANDER, ACCORDING TO CHARLES PEARS

He is an untiring worker, is blessed with more than his share of endurance, has a faculty for avoiding getting into "messes," and, should he be forced into them, has presence of mind and knowledge enough to get out of them with credit. His wants are simple; his thoughts are usually too sacred to bear expression by mere conversation.

THE SCHOONER-YACHT *EVADNE*, MALTA, MEDITERRANEAN SEA, FEBRUARY 22, 1870

The wind increased in violence till it blew a strong gale, sending us scudding along under close-reefed mainsail and jib. The hot blast of the sirocco made the atmosphere almost unbearable, but drove us along so well that at daylight on the morning of the 22nd we entered the harbour of Valetta, and by 6.30 a.m. were safely moored to one of the government buoys in French Creek. In the cutter a flying-fish was found dead, washed in during the night by one of the heavy seas which occasionally broke over us. We were fortunate to reach Malta when we did, as during the next four days it blew a violent gale, raising clouds of dust, which came sweeping from the shore across the harbour, covering the deck with sand, and driving locusts down the sky-lights into the cabins—visitors sufficiently unwelcome, yet better than the drenching seas we should have shipped had we encountered the storm far from a sheltering port.

—F. Trench Townshend

L. FRANCIS HERRESHOFF ON JOSHUA SLOCUM'S REBUILT OYSTER-DREDGER *SPRAY*

Spray was well named; she would spit spray all over you even in a light breeze and small sea if close hauled, and I think in a light breeze and chop of a sea could not go to windward. A great many people think *Spray* must have been a fine sea boat because of her long voyages, but the truth of the matter is she had none of the peculiarities of model which make seaworthiness.... The answer is the captain was a real genius at going to sea with poor gear. Such a man could make any boat steer herself and he would lay off courses so as to avoid beating to windward. He had been to sea many years and was a master at practical seamanship.

Joshua Slocum

Monday
17 PRESIDENT'S DAY

1886—The clipper ship *Young America*, renamed *Miroslav*, set sail from the Delaware River for Europe and was never heard from again.

Tuesday
18

1828—A powerful storm struck Gibraltar; more than 100 vessels were destroyed.

Wednesday
19

1845—The first metal buoys—riveted iron barrels—as aids to navigation were put into service for the first time, replacing barrels of wooden stave construction.

Thursday
20

1844—Joshua Slocum, the first person to sail around the world singlehanded, was born in North Mountain, Annapolis County, Nova Scotia.

Friday
21

1849—A design for a U.S. yacht ensign, which had been developed by the New York Yacht Club, was approved by the Secretary of the Navy.

Saturday
22 WASHINGTON'S BIRTHDAY

1857—Robert Baden-Powell, founder of the Boy Scout movement, was born in London, England.

Sunday
23

1822—The U.S. Congress authorized the use of revenue cutters to prevent the illegal cutting of live oaks, a superior shipbuilding timber, on public lands in Florida.

YOUR CHOICE

Fools build yachts for wise men to buy.
—OR—
Wise men build yachts for fools to buy.

It is easier to buy a boat than to sell one.
—William Atkin

CHOOSING A BOAT, ACCORDING TO VANDERDECKEN

Begin with a small craft, because thereby at small expense you will be enabled to judge whether the sea and its pastimes suit you, not only in a physical, but in a pecuniary point of view. Buy, don't build. Ships are like bricks and mortar; once you get into them, it is remarkably hard work to get out. There are plenty of small vessels suitable to a beginner always to be had. Do not bother your head about speed; if it can be obtained of course so much the better. As to appearance, a pint of paint, a pound of putty, and a few particles of good taste will convert a lumbering-looking shrimper into a regular Mosquito clipper.

A FEW OPTIONS IF YOU MUST HAVE A YACHT THAT IS TOO LARGE FOR YOUR MEANS

1. Buy and maintain her in partnership with one or two others.
2. Charter her out for part of the season.
3. Use her one season, charter her out for the next.

THE U.S. FLAGSHIP *LANCASTER*, OFF THE CAPE OF GOOD HOPE, FEBRUARY 24, 1887

All necessary stores being on board we left Table Bay at 2:10 P. M. bound for the south-western end of the Island of Madagascar to investigate the loss of an American barque, the *Surprise*, which went ashore on a reef about sixty miles north of Tullear Bay in a fog, in November, 1885.... After steaming clear of land we swung ship for compass deviations, and as pure and white as the driven snow was the Table Cloth on Table Mountain as we passed.

Farewell to Cape Town, and here let us say,
We expect to be back by the middle of May;
Then the people will flock to the Alfred Dock
To visit the ship and hear our band play.

We encountered strong head winds, and that night some of the watch declared they saw the phantom ship of old Vanderdecken, the "Flying Dutchman," trying to weather the "Stormy Cape."
—Lorenzo Hoag

BUT CONSIDER THIS ADVICE FROM WILLIAM WINN

If you have a boat, be greedy and have it all to yourself. If you cannot afford a large one, content yourself with a small one. If you can't afford to keep one at all, wait for an invitation from some one who can; but take my advice and never go into partnership in a boat, for you are sure to fall out. You will perpetually be called upon to pay the piper for pleasures in which you have not participated.

I know a cure for everything. Salt water.
                              —Isak Dinesen

FEB/MARCH

Monday
24

1925—Three charges of Thermit—powdered aluminum and oxide of iron—were ignited to break up a huge ice jam in the St. Lawrence River at Waddington, New York; this was the first time Thermit was so used.

Tuesday
25

1945—The Coast Guard icebreaker *Northwind,* the first ship to make the Northwest Passage in both directions, was launched in San Pedro, California.

Wednesday
26

1942—Aviator Don Mason, U.S. Navy, sent one of the most famous and succinct messages of World War II: "Sighted sub sank same."

Thursday
27

1977—The first *Pride of Baltimore,* a replica of a Baltimore clipper, was launched in the Inner Harbor of Baltimore, Maryland.

Friday
28

1844—A large gun exploded aboard the USS *Princeton,* which was carrying the president of the United States and several members of his cabinet on a Potomac River excursion; the secretaries of state and navy, among others, were killed.

Saturday
1

2003—Administrative control of the U.S. Coast Guard was transferred by Congress to the newly created Department of Homeland Security from the Department of Transportation.

Sunday
2

There is a sublime uncertainty about a sailing boat
                              —William Forwell

THE SCIENTIFIC RESEARCH SHIP *CHALLENGER*, ATLANTIC OCEAN NEAR THE WEST INDIES, MARCH 5, 1873

We were surrounded by gulf-weed, which a boat went away to examine, and picked up small shrimps, snails, crabs, and round little fish which make nests of the weed, cementing them by some glutinous substance, and then hang on outside by two absurd little arm-fins and fingers. The crabs are frequently found in possession of these fish-nests. In the next haul from 2,435 fms., we got three shark's teeth and a few phosphate secretions; and in the next—2,650 fms., on dark-red clay bottom—a small eel. Shoals of dolphin swam round the ship, their young, and the young of flying fish, being caught in the towing net. We saw great numbers of these gulf-weed fish-nests; it is curious how the animals which live among the weed correspond to it exactly in colour—shrimps, snails, and fish. The "phosphate secretions" turn out on analysis to be manganese.... and the question is why at these great depths do dead things become covered and impregnated with manganese?

—Lord George Campbell

HOLYSTONING THE DECKS

Holystones, also known as ecclesiastical bricks, were used to clean and smooth wooden decks. The larger stones, used for open spaces, were called "bibles." The smaller ones, for getting into corners and working along the edges of the deck furniture and the rails, were called "prayer books." The specific act of holystoning, wherein the sailors got down on their hands and knees with the stones, was known as "praying."

Holystoning was hard work. "By having the fiddler to play to the men while stoning the decks," wrote Captain Francis Liardet in 1849, "I have invariably found that they have rubbed harder, and kept time to the music; this method will prevent that chit chat which you so often hear between the men while stoning the decks, their attention being quite taken up with their work and the music. It always struck me that the decks were better and sooner done in this manner, and the men in much better spirits."

Holystoning produced a handsome, snow-white surface on pine decks, but because the technique wore away at the wood, too much of it was generally forbidden. Instead, the men would clean the deck with scrapers, then brush it with a solution of loose sand and water.

Six days shalt thou labor
And do all thou art able,
And on the seventh,
Holystone the decks and scrape the cable.

—anon.

WOODEN DECK MAINTENANCE

Oil spots—Cover the spot overnight with a dollop of cornstarch. In the morning, sweep the spots clean. (The starch absorbs the oil.)

Bruises or dimples—Thoroughly wet the spot and the area around it. Lay a damp piece of canvas or heavy cloth over the spot and go over it with a hot laundry iron.

Mildew—Use a stiff brush to wash the surface thoroughly with a 3:1 solution of water and liquid bleach (Clorox).

Stubborn stains—Wash with a solution of 1 pound oxalic acid in 2 gallons warm, fresh water. Rinse the deck with salt water before the solution has a chance to dry.

Monday
3

1817—*Cleopatra's Barge*, considered to be the first American off-shore cruising yacht, got underway on her first voyage, from Salem, Massachusetts, to the Azores.

Tuesday
4

1977—Ensign Janna Lambine graduated from naval aviation training, thus becoming the first woman to qualify as an aircraft pilot in the U.S. Coast Guard.

Wednesday ○
5 ASH WEDNESDAY

1931—The U.S. Navy forbade the routine cleaning of wooden decks with holystones, which were wearing down the decks too quickly.

Thursday
6

1928—Captain Richard Woodget, skipper of the legendary tea clipper *Cutty Sark*, now preserved in Greenwich, England, died in Burnham Overy, Norfolk, England.

Friday
7

1774—The British Parliament passed a bill that forbade the landing of food and fuel in Boston until the East India Company was indemnified for the tea thrown overboard during the Boston Tea Party.

Saturday
8

1973—The U.S. Coast Guard cutter *Dauntless* seized a sportfishing vessel, the *Big L*, which was attempting to smuggle a ton of marijuana into the United States.

Sunday
9 DAYLIGHT SAVING TIME BEGINS

More people than one has any idea or have an inherited love of ships.
    —Basil Lubbock

I wonder that people who wanted to break the souls of heroes and martyrs never thought of sending them to sea and keeping them a little seasick.
                                    —Harriet Beecher Stowe

THESE THINGS ARE LIKELY TO BRING ON SEASICKNESS

Using binoculars for extended periods
Reading a book, especially one with fine
    print and especially when below decks
Remaining below decks, especially in the
    ends of the vessel where motion is greatest
Breathing engine fumes, especially diesel
Remaining next to someone smoking
    tobacco, especially cigars
Remaining next to someone who is seasick
Eating greasy, or heavy, or acidic foods
Drinking alcohol before embarking
Drinking coffee
Embarking when hungry, or tired, or thirsty,
    or otherwise out of sorts

When the breeze comes, and, with everything drawing below and aloft, you tear along ten or twelve knots an hour, the sensation of pleasure is complete—if you are not sick.
                                    —Sir Edward Sullivan

THE BARK-RIGGED AUXILIARY YACHT *GRIFFIN*, PORT OF ALEXANDRETTA, EASTERN MEDITERRANEAN, MARCH 14, 1881

What with walks, lawn-tennis, and dinner-parties, it was difficult to believe that we were anchored off the "most unwholesome port on the Syrian coast." The weather, too, was variable, fine weather alternating with storms and gales, smooth seas with rough and boisterous tempests. We were all invited on board the *Coquette*, where a large party of the consuls, their wives, sisters, and children, were assembled. Captain Burr had particularly requested that the children should not be brought; but I suppose the "not" had escaped the notice of the fond mothers, for they all were there. The most remarkable peculiarity of these foreign ladies was that they became sea-sick the moment they came on board, and in no way concealed their symptoms, but were very open in the expression of them. The men shouted, sang, and smoked cigarettes, and seemed to enjoy themselves very much. "Come to my cabin, we shall have a quiet talk," said Captain Burr to me; but, on his opening the door, there was a stout lady extended on his sofa, with a large bucket near her!
                                    —E. H. Maxwell

BUT IF YOU ARE, TRY THESE REMEDIES

Drink plenty of water
Eat saltines or other unflavored, dry, soda
    crackers
Keep your eyes on the horizon
Remain on deck in the fresh air
Keep warm on cold days and cool on hot days
Eat candied ginger, or drink ginger ale
Drink colas
Keep busy
Think positively

The captain of the *Pinafore*:
Though related to a peer,
I can hand, reef, and steer,
And ship a selvagee;
I am never known to quail
At the fury of a gale,
And I'm never, never sick at sea!
The crew:
What, never?
The captain:
No, never!
The crew:
What, never?
The captain:
Hardly ever!
                    —from "The Captain's Song," by W. S. Gilbert

MARCH

I'm on the sea! I'm on the sea!
I am where I would ever be.
—Bryan Waller Procter

Monday
10

A man's moral tone as well as his physical constitution improves by association with the sea.
—Captain A.J. Kenealy

Tuesday
11

1885—Malcolm Campbell, who would set several motorboat speed records, was born in Chislehurst, Kent, England.

Wednesday
12

1888—Two New York pilot boats—*Enchantress* and *Phantom*—were wrecked during the Great Blizzard of 1888.

Thursday ◐
13

1895—The Spanish cruiser *Reina Regente* sank off Gibraltar; 402 lives were lost.

Friday
14

1868—The Millwall Docks on the River Thames, London, were officially opened.

Saturday
15

1933—*In the Wake of the Bounty*, a film about the *Bounty* mutiny, with Errol Flynn in his film debut as Fletcher Christian, premiered in Sydney, Australia.

Sunday
16

1887—The New Zealand Amateur Rowing Association, a union of nine clubs, was established.

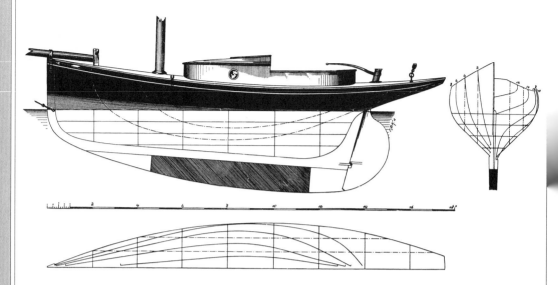

Within my mind there had been slowly taking shape, for years and years, the Perfect Ship. Every one knows her, I expect—that ship. In the minds of every sailor there float pictures of her, each one perfect, each one different.
—Weston Martyr

Somewhere there must lie a "perfect shape" for a yacht—one yielding maximum speed at all wind strengths, with windward ability to claw off a lee shore, able to care for the crew in the ultimate storm, and beautiful, too.
—Guy Cole

A ship's hull should be a beautifully symmetrical structure; and it is a remarkable fact that in shipbuilding admirable performance and beauty of appearance go hand in hand.
—Edwin Brett

One of a designer's most important requirements is an unerring eye for curves, and the ability to detect in them the least deviation from fairness.
—Douglas Phillips-Birt

Good draftsmanship is an aid to design, for it is the means of expression; nevertheless, a handsome set of plans does not insure a good design.
—Howard I. Chapelle

Shipmates, do not fool around with the designs of another man unless you are ready to accept the consequences, not only on the water but at the Pearly Gates.
—Robb White

Remember always that the simplest design is usually the best.... The more equipment and the more gadgets that are added means that there are that many more things to go wrong. Putting them right takes time and money.
—Francis S. Kinney

Less is more.
—Ludwig Mies van der Rohe

THE PILOT CUTTER *ESCAPE*, VIRGIN GORDA, CARIBBEAN SEA, MARCH 22–23, 1933

March 22nd.—Heavy squalls from S.E. during the night, but very little swell coming into the roadstead. Visited a Nova Scotia fishing schooner in the morning, taking a load of very fine ponies on board to ship to Barbadoes. H., the owner of the schooner a most interesting fellow, and one of the characters known all over the West Indies.

March 23rd.—Under way at 13.0. Nominally for Nassau in the Bahamas, but ready to call at any island that took our fancy. Loaded up with a cargo of vegetables and fruit, a kind present from R. the planter. Sailed over to watch the ponies swimming out to the schooner, and being hoisted aboard, a most exciting operation. Ran out of the Sound through Flanagan Pass. What a perfect cruising ground for a small boat and what lovely names. Ding-a-dong Nook, Dead Man's Chest, Treasure Point, Careening Cove, Fallen Jerusalem! Stevenson must have looked at this chart when writing "Treasure Island."
—D. W. Robertson

Do not judge the ship from the land.
—Italian proverb

MARCH

Monday
17 ST. PATRICKS DAY

1784—The House of Representatives of the Commonwealth of
Massachusetts voted to hang a "representation of a cod-fish in
the room where the House sit, as a memorial to the importance
of the cod-fishing to the welfare of the Commonwealth."

Tuesday
18

1921—The steamship *Hong Kong* sank in the South China Sea;
approximately 1,000 lives were lost.

Wednesday
19

1799—Britain's Royal Humane Society awarded a prize to
L. Granshaw for his method of throwing a line by bow and
arrow from ship to shore to rescue shipwrecked mariners.

Thursday
20 VERNAL EQUINOX

1929—The schooner *I'm Alone*, a rumrunner out of Nova Scotia,
was sunk off the east coast of the United States by gunfire from
the U.S. Coast Guard cutter *Dexter*.

Friday
21

1919—The U.S. Navy began testing the first gyrocompass, a Sperry.

Saturday
22

1893—The Oxford University crew defeated the
Cambridge University crew in the 50th running
of the Boat Race on the River Thames, England.

Sunday
23

1882—The U.S. Navy's Office of
Naval Intelligence was established.

EDITOR, WRITER, SAILOR

Thomas Fleming Day (1861–1927), the founding editor of *The Rudder*, began his working life as a manufacturer's representative, selling marine hardware, canoes, and other small craft. In 1891, recognizing a need for a magazine that was as much about boating as about yachting, he founded *The Rudder*. He felt strongly that too many boats spent too much time either at their moorings or sailing alongshore and that amateurs should sail offshore. To that end, in 1906 he organized the Bermuda Race. In 1911, to demonstrate that amateurs could easily take small cruising boats across the Atlantic Ocean, Day and a crew of two sailed from Newport, Rhode Island, to Gibraltar in the 32-foot yawl *Sea Bird*, designed by Charles Mower and himself. The next year, to demonstrate the reliability of the internal combustion engine for marine use, he and a crew of three took the 35-foot motorboat *Detroit* from New York to St. Petersburg, Russia. In 1917 he retired from The *Rudder* and opened a yacht chandlery in New York City. With a nod to Dante, a sign on the wall there proclaimed to customers: "Give Up All Hope Ye Who Enter Here."

THE OCEANOGRAPHIC RESEARCH SHIP *CHALLENGER*, NEAR THE VIRGIN ISLANDS, CARIBBEAN SEA, MARCH 24–25, 1873

During the operation of heaving in the dredge a fatal accident occurred, by the parting of a rope span used for securing the iron leading block for the dredge-rope, which in its flight across the deck struck a seaman, named William Stokes, so severely on the head as to produce concussion of the brain, from which he died in a few hours.... After evening quarters, the bell tolled, and all the ship's company assembled to pay their last tribute to their late shipmate. The captain read the beautiful and appropriate service for a burial at sea, and on reaching that portion, "We commit his body to the deep," it was slid out of the port, wrapped in a hammock weighted with shot, into the bright blue tide, to be seen no more until that day when the sea shall give up its dead.

—W. J. J. Spry

WHEN
by Thomas Fleming Day

When western winds are blowing soft
    Across the Island Sound;
When every sail that draws aloft
    Is swollen true and round;
When yellow shores along the lee
    Slope upward to the sky;
When opal bright the land and sea
    In changeful contact lie;
When idle yachts at anchor swim
    Above a phantom shape;
When spires of canvas dot the rim
    Which curves from cape to cape;
When sea-weed strewn the ebbing tide
    Pours eastward to the main;
When clumsy coasters side by side
    Tack in and out again—
When such a day is mine to live,
    What has the world beyond to give?

*I know of nothing that will so set a man's blood
flowing like a fight with a wind-mad sail.*
                                    —Thomas Fleming Day

MARCH

Monday
24

1827—Donald McKay, a recent immigrant from Nova Scotia
who would build some of the greatest clipper ships, became
apprenticed to Isaac Webb, shipbuilder, of New York City.

Tuesday
25

1853—The extreme clipper ship *Belle of the West*, designed
by Samuel Pook and built by Shiverick Bros., was launched
in East Dennis, Massachusetts.

Wednesday
26

1853—In an hour, in the vicinity of Boston, at the zenith
of clipper-ship construction, five clippers were launched:
John Land, West Wind, White Swallow, Star of Empire,
and *Queen of Clippers.*

Thursday
27

1861—Thomas Fleming Day, founding editor of *The Rudder*
magazine, was born in Somersetshire, England.

Friday
28

Two U.S. Navy battleships—*Iowa* (1896) and *Oklahoma* (1914)—
were launched on this day.

Saturday
29

1968—Hugo Vihlen set sail from Casablanca
to attempt a crossing of the Atlantic in the
5-foot 11 $^1/_2$-inch sloop *April Fool*.

Sunday
30

1899—The United Fruit Company,
known as the Banana Navy for its great
fleet of freighters, was established.

Sailors work like horses at sea and spend their money like asses ashore.

—anon.

And now the storm is over,
And we are safe and well;
We will walk into a public house
And drink and drink our fill;
We will drink strong ale and porter,
And we'll make the rafters roar,
And when our money is all spent
We'll be off to sea once more!

—from a halyard chantey

FOUR COMMONLY PERCEIVED PRINCIPAL DESIRES OF JOLLY JACK TAR, THE SAILORMAN

Women
Tobacco
Rum
More rum
(not necessarily in that
    order)

I yam what I yam.
—Popeye

Sailors will never be convinced that rum is a dangerous thing, by taking it away from them, and giving it to the officers.
—Richard Henry Dana

SLIGHTLY DRUNK, IN THE WORDS OF THE SAILOR

Half seas over
Half a brick in his hat
Trimmed down
Shaking a cloth in the wind

DRUNK

Bonkers
Cockbilled
Sewn up
Stitched
Under full sail

REALLY, REALLY DRUNK

Deado
Anchored in Sot's Bay
Three sheets to the wind
Back teeth awash

THE U.S. STEAM SLOOP-OF-WAR *BROOKLYN*, AT ANCHOR, MONTEVIDEO, URUGUAY, MARCH 31, 1882

Forty-eight hours' liberty was given to the starboard watch. As this was the first "general liberty" granted since the ship went into commission, it of course occasioned considerable excitement among the men, and this excitement became so intense soon after their arrival on shore that the Uruguayan authorities found it necessary to invite several of the most demonstrative to the cabildo, where they were permitted to remain until they cooled off. When the men finally got back to the ship, the events which had occurred during the "general liberty" were thoroughly discussed, and many wild and thrilling yarns were told. One sailor found a coat lying in the street, about two o'clock in the morning, and thought he had found a prize, but was soon afterwards arrested for stealing. When his case came up in court, he explained to the court that he was from Ohio, and the judge promptly released him, recognizing the well-known fact that people in Ohio generally "take things," political offices included.

—Lieutenant W. H. Beehler, USN

*The sea is the same as it has been since
before men ever went on it in boats.*
—Ernest Hemingway

MARCH/APRIL

Monday
31

1909—The keel of the White Star liner RMS *Titanic* was laid in Belfast, Ireland.

Tuesday
1

1960—A new numbering system for undocumented motorboats on navigable waters was established by the U.S. Coast Guard.

Wednesday
2

1982—Argentinian forces invaded the British-held Falkland Islands in the South Atlantic, precipitating the first large-scale naval war since World War II.

Thursday
3

1798—Charles Wilkes, commander of the United States Exploring Expedition of 1838–42, also known as the Wilkes Expedition, was born in New York City.

Friday
4

The mere sight of the sea has an attraction to the true son of Neptune as cogent as that of the magnet to the pole.
                                        —Captain A. J. Kenealy

Saturday
5

1804—The first semipermanent wooden pontoon bridge—squared-off pine timbers over pine logs—was built across Collins Pond, Lynn, Massachusetts, by Captain Moses Brown.

Sunday
6

1609—Henry Hudson set sail from Texel Island, Holland, aboard the *Halve Maen* (Half Moon) on a voyage of exploration that would lead to the discovery of the Hudson River.

THE ART OF DESIGN

Perhaps the greatest yacht designer of the 20th century, Olin J. Stephens II (1908–2008) created a long string of memorable designs, among them these racing and cruising legends:

Ocean racers—*Dorade, Stormy Weather, Bolero, Baruna, Finisterre, Palawan, Brilliant*
Cruising yachts—Hinckley Islander, Hinckley Pilot, Tartan, Weekender
America's Cup defenders—*Intrepid, Columbia, Constellation, Courageous, Freedom*
Racing classes—Lightning, Blue Jay, Shields, Interclub, Cape Cod Mercury

Mostly self-taught—he attended the Massachusetts Institute of Technology for only one semester—Stephens was an intuitive designer: an artist rather than an engineer. He nevertheless was one of the pioneers in the use of testing tanks to study the behavior of scale models in varying conditions. Evolution, not revolution, was his game. One design would lead logically to another, and then another and another, eventually resulting in yachts that were faster, more seaworthy, and more beautiful than those of the competition. For example, his first 12-meter yacht, *Vim*, hugely successful in its own right, became the lead boat in a line of successful America's Cup defenders that, through observational refinement, led to *Intrepid*, considered by most observers to have been the greatest 12-meter ever built.

I can't really remember a time I didn't want to design boats.
—Olin J. Stephens II

ON BECOMING A YACHT DESIGNER

The quickest way to learn boat drawing is to draw or copy drawings, continue the practice until every point and line and their meanings is indelibly fixed in the mind. No one may expect to master the subject by simply reading it over—It requires *study* and *practice*.
—C. P. Kunhardt

It is not enough that a yacht should be weatherly, smart, and efficient. She should be beautiful and appealing, not to the eye alone, but to the heart as well.
—Hervey Garrett Smith

THE OYSTER SLOOP *SPRAY*, SOUTH ATLANTIC OCEAN, APRIL 11, 1898

I was awakened by that rare bird, the booby, with its harsh quack, which I recognized at once as a call to go on deck; it was as much as to say, "Skipper, there's land in sight." I tumbled out quickly, and sure enough, away ahead in the dim twilight, about twenty miles off, was St. Helena. My first impulse was to call out, "Oh, what a speck in the sea!" It is in reality nine miles in length and two thousand eight hundred and twenty-three feet in height. I reached for a bottle of port-wine out of the locker, and took a long pull from it to the health of my invisible helmsman—the pilot of the *Pinta*.
—Joshua Slocum

My boat breathes sturdy, eager confidence, a living embodiment of the truth that the sea is for sailing.
—H. W. Tilman

APRIL

Monday
7

1922—An automatic steering gear, aka "Gyropilot," aka "Metalmike," was installed in a commercial ship, the *John D. Archibold*, for the first time.

Tuesday
8

1861—The extreme clipper ship *Witchcraft* drove ashore at Chickamaconic, North Carolina; 15 lives were lost.

Wednesday
9

1866—Several thousand ship carpenters and other shipyard workers in Greenport, Long Island, New York, began a six-week strike for an eight-hour day.

Thursday
10

1881—The ferry *Princess Victoria* sank in the Thames River, Ontario, Canada; 180 lives were lost.

Friday ◐
11

1921—Telephone service via underwater cable was established between Key West, Florida, and Havana, Cuba.

Saturday
12

1921—The fishing schooner *Mayflower*, designed by Starling Burgess to compete in the International Fishermen's Races but disqualified because of her yachtlike design, was launched in Essex, Massachusetts.

Sunday
13 PALM SUNDAY

1908—Olin J. Stephens II, yacht designer, was born in New York.

SOLID ADVICE ON BOATBUILDING TOOLS FROM R. D. "PETE" CULLER

In this age of motorization of everything, including tooth brushes, we tend to lose sight of some of the basics. Boatbuilding tools should not be motorized gadgets. If a power tool will save a lot of time, by all means use it. Hand tools certainly still have their place. What is needed is a basic assortment of high-quality hand and power tools.

CROSSCUT SAWS FOR BOAT CARPENTRY

All-around use—26-inch blade, 8 or 9 teeth to the inch

Fine joinerwork—24-inch blade, 11 or 12 teeth to the inch

HAND PLANES FOR BOAT CARPENTRY

9-inch smooth plane for general use
6-inch block plane
Bullnose plane for working in corners

TWO ADVISEMENTS FOR THE WOODEN BOAT BUILDER TO LIVE BY

Measure twice, cut once.
Always cut on the wastewood side.

AND ANOTHER, FROM WILLIAM ATKIN

Sooner or later, whether you do the work yourself or hire someone to do it, a truck will roll up and unload a pile of lumber. The cedar will perfume the place, and before you know it folks will be stopping in to tell you how "they" would do the job. Close, then, your ears to these, and stick to the plans.

THE MACKEREL SEINER *MOOWEEN*, ATLANTIC OCEAN SOUTHWEST OF MARTHA'S VINEYARD, APRIL 20, 1906

About 9:30 at night the writer jumped out of his berth in response to the cry, "All hands in the boat." I got into my oilers and boots as quickly as possible and rushed on deck. The night was black, so black one could not see his hand in front of his face. The skipper was aloft, for I could hear his voice calling out to us to hurry. Finally we were all in the boat, thirteen of us, nine rowers, the seine heaver, the bight passer, the cork heaver and the steersman, when suddenly the skipper said, "There's a school on our weather. See it?" .... The writer glanced in the direction indicated and saw a great white phosphorescent spot on the water, just like a great white sheet. That was the school. Well, we started pulling for it but had only gone a short distance when the Captain sung out, "It's gone down. Come back to the vessel." And so we lost the first school we saw.... When we finally got back alongside, instead of going aboard, a towing-line was passed to us and we towed astern for several hours hoping that another school would show up. But none did.

—John E. Graham

Building a small wooden boat for the first time takes the would-be builder into unknown territory.
—John Gardner

APRIL

Monday
14 PASSOVER

1528—A Spanish expedition to Florida led by Pánfilo de Narváez began to build five boats, the first constructed by Europeans in America.

Tuesday
15

1996—Stavros Spyros Niarchos, billionaire ship owner, died in Zurich, Switzerland.

Wednesday
16

1947—The French freighter *Grandcamp*, loaded with nitrates, caught fire and exploded in Texas City, Texas, destroying herself and the cargo ship *Highflyer* and leveling most of the city; more than 500 lives were lost.

Thursday
17

1893—A weeklong great rendezvous of naval ships from the United States, Britain, France, Spain, Italy, Germany, Russia, Brazil, and Holland got underway at Hampton Roads, Virginia.

Friday
18 GOOD FRIDAY

1848—A U.S. Navy expedition to explore the inland waters of the Middle East, commanded by Lieutenant William F. Lynch, reached the Dead Sea.

Saturday
19

1866—The *Agamemnon* of Liverpool's Blue Funnel Line, the first steam-powered freighter to compete with the sailing tea clippers, got underway from Liverpool on her first voyage to China.

Sunday
20 EASTER SUNDAY

1893—The British royal yacht *Britannia*, a gaff-rigged cutter designed by George Lennox Watson, was launched at the D&W Henderson Yard on the River Clyde, Scotland.

THE SCHOONER *UPOLU*, OFF THE COAST OF QUEENSLAND, AUSTRALIA, APRIL 24, 1886

At nine o'clock in the morning, the sun shone out, making everything appear bright and cheerful. The sea water was as clear and translucent as sea water ever is, out in those tropical climates, so that if there had been no wind we should have seen right down, down—well, I do not know how deep. As it was, in spite of the surface ripple, there seemed to be something white below the soft green of the tropical waves which looked strange to us, leaning over the side of the ship. Presently, after gazing for some time, it seemed to approach nearer. Then we suddenly became aware that it was the glistening, uneven surface of white coral.... I thought of telling the drowsy captain just what I saw beneath the ship, but he had been so much annoyed the day before, when I made some remarks a-propos of his sailing, that I concluded to keep quiet and calmly pray for a happy ending.... Presently there was a great crash, followed by a dismal grating sound. We had been going through the water at nearly seven knots an hour, but now all was still, especially the ship, which had come to a conclusion on the reef.

—a member of the crew

SAILING AMONG REEFS

For better visibility, try to sail with the sun astern. Light green shades indicate deeper water; dark green indicates shallower water.

When a boat goes aground, mother nature has spoken. —anon.

Only two sailors, in my experience, never ran aground. One never left port and the other was an atrocious liar.
—Don Bamford

TO GET OFF THE GROUND

If under power and aground on a sandy bottom, do not use full throttle, as the suck of the propeller is liable to throw sand under the boat, making her more firmly aground.

Get an anchor out to deeper water. Try to pull the boat toward the anchor.

If aground by the bow, move the crew to the stern; if aground by the stern, move the crew to the bow; if aground amidships, try to roll her off by swaying on the rigging or running the crew from side to side.

Heel the boat by backing the jib and having the crew lean out on the lee shrouds. The draft can be reduced by nearly a third if the boat can be heeled as much as 45 degrees.

Or try this: Fill the dinghy with water and secure it to the end of the main boom. Swing the boom out as far as it will go. Take up on the main topping lift. The weight of the dinghy will heel the boat.

Sometimes having the crew jump up and down in unison can shake her off.

*I have known the sea too long to
believe in its respect for decency.*
—Joseph Conrad

APRIL

Monday
21

1906—The *Governor Cobb*, the first oceangoing merchant
vessel to be powered by a steam turbine, was launched in
Chester, Pennsylvania.

Tuesday
22

1862—The American Shipmasters' Association, now known
as the American Bureau of Shipping, was incorporated in
New York.

Wednesday
23

1918—The bark *Bertha*, the last whaleship built in New
Bedford, Massachusetts, was lost at sea while engaged
in the packet trade between the Cape Verde Islands and
New Bedford.

Thursday
24

1999—The catamaran *Playstation*, which a month
previously set a record to date for a day's run of 580.23
miles, burned at its dock in Auckland, New Zealand.

Friday ◐
25

1874—Guglielmo Marconi, the father of wireless telegraphy
and the first person to successfully send a wireless signal
across the Atlantic Ocean, was born in Bologna, Italy.

Saturday
26

1869—The Portland Yacht Club, the third oldest
continuously operating yacht club in the United
States, was founded in Portland, Maine.

Sunday
27

1969—David Pyle and a crew of one set sail
from England in the 18-foot Drascombe lugger
Hermes, arriving in Australia 341 days later at
the end of the longest open-boat cruise to date.

THE "ROMANCE" OF WHALING

As soon as her anchor was down we went aboard, and found her to be the whale-ship, *Wilmington and Liverpool Packet*, of New Bedford, last from the "off-shore ground," with nineteen hundred barrels of oil. A "spouter" we knew her to be as soon as we saw her, by her cranes and boats, and by her stump topgallant masts, and a certain slovenly look to the sails, rigging, spars, and hull…. Her rigging was slack and turning white; no paint on the spars or blocks; clumsy seizings and straps without covers, and homeward bound splices in every direction. Her crew, too, were not in much better order. Her captain was a Quaker, in a suit of brown, with a broad-rimmed hat, and sneaking about decks like a sheep, with his head down.

—Richard Henry Dana, Jr.

The reducing of leviathan to merchantable elements is one of the most knock-down processes in the smelly line that the human senses can meet with.

—C. Fox Smith

J. O. DAVIDSON

THE STEAM WHALER *ARCTIC*, DUNDEE, SCOTLAND, MAY 2, 1873

Having arranged terms with her wealthy and prosperous owners, I found myself installed on board, having signed articles as second mate to the effect that I engaged myself "to serve on board the good ship 'Arctic' on a voyage from Dundee to Greenland or Davis' Straits, and seas adjacent, for whale and for other fishing, and back to Dundee;" and, further, that I agreed to "conduct myself in an orderly, faithful, honest, and sober manner, and to be at all times diligent in my respective duties, and to be obedient to the lawful commands of my said master." The daily allowance which I should receive of butter, cheese, oatmeal, bread, beef, pork, flour, tea, sugar, lemon-juice, water, and other stores, were previously read to myself and the whole crew at the shipping office. My wages were to be one shilling per month, and I was to receive in addition the sum of one penny for every ton of oil brought home in the ship, and one farthing for every ton of whalebone.

—Albert Hastings Markham

A WHALEBOAT'S CREW

Mate (also known as the Boatheader)—In charge of the boat; steers while approaching the whale; once the whale has been harpooned, goes forward and kills the whale with a lance.

Boatsteerer (also the Harpooner)—Pulls the forward oar; throws the harpoon; steers when the mate goes forward to lance the whale.

Bowman—Pulls the second oar; tends the whaleline after the whale has been harpooned.

Midship oarsman—Pulls the third oar.

Tub oarsman—Pulls the fourth oar, also known as the tub oar; keeps the whaleline wet to keep it cool as the whale sounds.

After oarsman—Pulls the stroke oar; coils the whaleline as it is brought aboard; bails the boat.

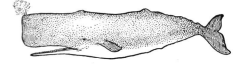

*The sea has a rude pistolling sort of odour,
that takes you in the nostrils like snuff.*
—Robert Louis Stevenson

APRIL/MAY

Monday
28

1865—In the worst maritime disaster in U.S. history, the Mississippi River steamboat *Sultana* exploded and burned; 1,700 lives—nearly all Union soldiers returning home—were lost.

Tuesday
29

1859—Construction officially began, at Port Said, Egypt, on a ship canal, the Suez, that would eventually connect the Mediterranean and Red Seas.

Wednesday
30

1853—The clipper ship *Young America*, designed and built by William H. Webb, was launched in New York City.

Thursday
1

1988—Ben Lexcen, born Robert Miller, designer of the winged keel that was instrumental in *Australia II*'s becoming the first non-American yacht to win the America's Cup, died in Sydney, Australia.

Friday
2

1827—The first steam ferryboat in Detroit, Michigan, went into service.

Saturday ○
3

1856—The British government removed many of the descendants of the HMS *Bounty* mutineers from Pitcairn Island, which had become overcrowded, to Norfolk Island.

Sunday
4

1904—The United States took formal possession from the French of the site and property of what would become the Panama Canal.

A TOPSAIL SCHOONER AMONG THE SOUTH PACIFIC ISLANDS, MAY 11, 1873

On Sunday we sighted Rotumah. This was the first island I intended visiting, my object here being to ship some of the natives, to strengthen my present crew. No one ought to attempt a voyage through the South Sea Islands without carrying an extra crew of this kind.... We got up to the land in the afternoon, and rounding the north-east end of the island, ran close past a small islet called Hama, and dropped anchor in fourteen fathoms, the small islet bearing east by north, about half a mile distant—the main land about a mile and a-half. This is the best anchorage at Rotumah, but though well protected from the prevailing south-east trade-winds it is by no means a snug one, for should the wind fly round to the north, it is better to get up the anchor and stand out to sea at once, rather than wait till a northerly swell comes rolling in, with the dirty, unsettled weather that usually accompanies a wind from that quarter.

—C. F. Wood

PAINTING AND VARNISHING—NOTES FROM *THE RUDDER*, 1916, STILL PERTINENT TODAY

It is not always necessary to remove all the old varnish, but just lightly sandpaper the surface before putting on the new coat.

If the old surface is black and stained, it should be taken off with some reliable varnish remover and the wood bleached with oxalic acid. When using the latter wear rubber gloves or else apply with a swab tied on a stick. After the acid has dried, sandpaper the surface of the wood.

Start painting and varnishing fairly early in the morning in order that it may set naturally in the warmth of the day. A northwest wind makes a perfect day for varnishing.

Sudden chilling of nightfall may ruin freshly applied coatings, particularly varnish, by causing them to crack.

Always varnish before painting, because if you do the painted parts first and then try to varnish where the paint has run over the line and soaked into the pores of the wood, it will always look badly. But any varnish that runs over the line can be painted over. It is easy to remove wet paint from a varnished surface.

If you're going to paint, paint as if you mean it. None of this dip and dab business; paint with the paint—load your brush up and go at it.
—Dynamite Payson

VARNISH RECIPES FROM THE OLD DAYS WHEN SAILORS MIXED THEIR OWN, ACCORDING TO DIXON KEMP

Oak varnish—7 pounds pale resin dissolved in 2 gallons oil of turpentine.

Quick-drying varnish—7 pounds copal (a type of resin), hot linseed 1/2 gallon, hot turpentine 1.5 gallons. Carefully stir and boil together.

Quick-drying varnish for metals—powder 1 pound of copal and dissolve in 2 pounds of strongest alcohol.

Black varnish or polish for iron—resin 4 ounces, lamp black 2 ounces, beeswax 3 ounces, shellac 2 ounces, linseed oil 1 quart. Boil together one hour, and then stir in 1/2 pint turpentine.

A sailing vessel is alive in a way that no ship with mechanical power can ever be.
—Aubrey de Selincourt

MAY

Monday
5 BANK HOLIDAY / UK

1998—Philip Rhodes, yacht designer, died in Middletown, Connecticut.

Tuesday
6

1862—Henry David Thoreau, author of *Cape Cod* and *A Week on the Concord and Merrimack Rivers*, died in Concord, Massachusetts.

Wednesday
7

1905—Ten ocean liners arrived in New York Harbor on this day with a total of 12,039 immigrants on board, a record number; most of the immigrants were from Italy.

Thursday
8

No Socks Day
(shoes optional)

Friday
9

1894—The Canadian revenue cutter *Petrel* seized two American steamboats on Lake Erie and arrested the crews for illegal fishing in Canadian waters.

Saturday
10

1877—The Great Salt Lake Yacht Club, Utah, was established.

Sunday
11 MOTHER'S DAY / US & CANADA

1960—The *France*, the last major transatlantic passenger liner to be built for the French Line, was launched at St. Nazaire, France.

THIS IS WHAT WE SAW OFF THE COAST OF NOVA SCOTIA IN 1833

We beheld at the distance of from 150 to 200 yards on our starboard bow, the head and neck of some denizen of the deep.... We were, of course, all taken aback at the sight, and with staring eyes and in speechless wonder stood gazing at it for full half a minute: there could be no mistake, no delusion, and we were all perfectly satisfied that we had been favored with a view of the "true and veritable sea serpent," which had been generally considered to have existed only in the brain of some Yankee skipper, and treated as a tale not much entitled to belief.

—from the sworn testimony of five British army officers

THE SEA SNAKE, ACCORDING TO SIR WALTER SCOTT

The sea-snake...arising out of the depths of ocean, stretches to the skies his enormous neck, covered with a mane like that of a war-horse, and, with his broad glittering eyes raised masthead high, looks out, as it seems, for plunder or for victims.

THE SEA SERPENT

by Oliver Herford

O wondrous worm that won
   the Height
Of Fame by keeping out of
   sight!
Never was known on Land
   or Sea
Such a Colossal Modesty;
Never such arrogant pre-
   tence
Of Ostentatious Diffidence.
Celebrity whom none has
   seen,
Save some Post Prandial
   Marine,
No magazine can repro-
   duce
Your Photograph.—Oh,
   what's the use
Of doing things when one
   may be
So Famous a Nonentity!

THE YAWL *KITTIE*, BUZZARDS BAY, MASSACHUSETTS, MAY 16, 1892

At daylight I awoke, looked out and saw that it was blowing very hard from the Southwest. This wind, especially with an ebb-tide, makes a very nasty sea, as it blows right into Buzzards Bay from the Atlantic Ocean. Lou was sleeping soundly and as he was a youngster I let him snooze, made myself a cup of coffee, which with some fried ham and eggs made me a good breakfast and quite comfortable, as where the yawl was anchored [in Cuttyhunk Island harbor] was smooth as a millpond. After stowing things away carefully, I tumbled up on deck, turned in three reefs in the mainsail, one reef in the mizzen sail and set a small jib, got underway by myself, bringing the anchor and rode into the cockpit.... As I stood across Buzzards Bay on the port tack and got clear of Cuttyhunk, the sea came in heavy and kept me busy. I ran about halfway across the bay, came about standing well out by the Sow and Pigs Lightship on the starboard tack, so when I came about again on the port tack I would have a good offing.

—Hazen Morse

Sailors have much superstition, but little sentiment.
—Aubrey de Selincourt

MAY

Monday
12

1792—Captain Robert Gray discovered a great river on the north-west coast of America, naming it after his ship, the *Columbia*.

Tuesday
13

1888—Captain Joshua Slocum launched the 35-foot sailing canoe *Liberdade*, which he built himself on a beach in Brazil to carry him and his family back to the United States after having been shipwrecked.

Wednesday
14

1934—The yawl *Stormy Weather*, designed by Olin Stephens II and one of the winningest yachts of her day, was launched at the Henry B. Nevins Yard, City Island, New York.

Thursday
15

1833—Five officers of the British army, on a fishing expedition out of Halifax, Nova Scotia, spotted a giant sea serpent.

Friday
16

1887—The Lake Champlain Yacht Club was established in Burlington, Vermont.

Saturday
17

1849—The steamboat *White Cloud* caught fire at St. Louis, Missouri; the fire spread to 22 other steamboats, 3 barges, and 1 canal boat, destroying them, and to the city itself, burning 15 city blocks.

Sunday
18

1845—HMS *Erebus* and HMS *Terror*, commanded by Sir John Franklin, set sail from England in search of the Northwest Passage; they never returned, nor did their crews.

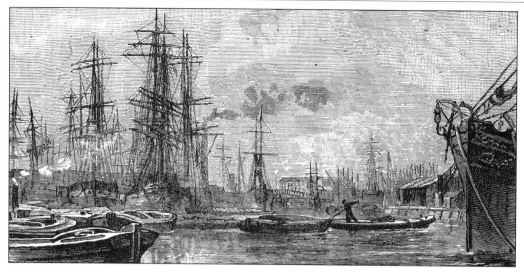

A FEW U.S. FIRSTS

First practical underwater telegraph cable—across the Hudson River between Fort Lee, New Jersey, and New York City, by Ezra Cornell, 1845

First pleasure yacht—*Jefferson*, a 35-foot sloop constructed by Christopher Turner for Captain George Crowninshield, Salem, Massachusetts, 1801

First canal—built around falls in the Connecticut River at South Hadley, Massachusetts, by Benjamin Prescott

First lighthouse illuminated by natural gas—Barcelona Harbor, Lake Erie, New York, 1830

First National Seashore—Cape Hatteras (North Carolina) National Seashore, 1937

First naval aircraft—Curtiss Amphibian Triad, delivered 1911

First novel about whaling—*Miriam Coffin; or, The Whale-Fishermen*, by Joseph C. Hart, 1842

First coast pilot book—*The American Coast Pilot*, by Captain Lawrence Furlong, published in Newburyport, Massachusetts, 1796

First scheduled coastal shipping service—five packet ships owned by Thomas Lowery Servoss that ran between New York City and New Orleans, 1831

First salt works based on the evaporation of seawater—Accomack, Virginia, 1630

First ice exported—130 tons from Boston to Martinique, aboard the brig *Favorite*, 1805

First lifesaving service—Humane Society of the Commonwealth of Massachusetts, 1787

First lifeboat for a lifesaving service—surfboat built in Nantucket, Massachusetts, by William Raymond for the Humane Society of the Commonwealth of Massachusetts

First steamship deck chair—introduced by the Ocean Comfort Company, 1891

First wire rope factory—Saxonburg, Pennsylvania, 1841

First commercial varnish manufacturer—Christian Schrack, Philadelphia, Pennsylvania, 1815

First periscope—invented by Thomas Doughty, Acting Chief Engineer, U.S. Navy, 1864

First naval radio station—Navesink, New Jersey, 1903

First oceanography institution—Scripps Institution of Oceanography, University of California, La Jolla, California, originally the Scripps Institution for Biological Research, established in 1912

THE SCHOONER KAALOKAI, AMONG THE HAWAIIAN ISLANDS, MAY 24, 1891

After rounding Barber's Point we stood well out towards the center of Kauai channel, to avoid the calms which occasionally prevail on the southwest part of Oahu. On reaching the center it fell calm, but soon a nasty sea got up, short but heavy. Towards evening it looked as though we were going to have a disagreeable time of it, and so we did; gusts of wind would come, with rain and more sea, then calm again, then a heavy squall would fetch us and send us beam into the sea. Our little craft, close reefed down, however, stood it well; at one moment our bowsprit would be pointing towards heaven and the next few seconds the jibboom would be investigating the depths of the sea. Having everything secure and hove to under the closereefed foresail, we went below and blessed the composer of "Blow high ye winds." We were all as sick as cats. It rained all night on deck, and down below it reigned confusion.
                                    —Captain F. D. Walker

Monday
19 VICTORIA DAY / CANADA

1912—The first U.S.-directed North Atlantic ice patrol to protect shipping from icebergs got underway; it would be superseded two years later by the International Ice Patrol.

Tuesday
20

1498—Vasco da Gama, Portuguese navigator, landed at Calicut on the Malabar Coast, thus becoming the first European to round the Cape of Good Hope and cross the Indian Ocean.

Wednesday
21

1829—The cornerstone was laid for the U.S. Navy's Boston Dry Dock, Charlestown, Massachusetts, the first of the type to be built by the federal government.

Thursday
22

1902—Maurice Griffiths, author, yacht designer, editor of *Yachting Monthly*, was born in South London, England.

Friday
23

1904—A Gold Cup symbolizing supremacy in the new sport of autoboat racing was deeded to the Larchmont Yacht Club of Rye, New York.

Saturday
24

1799—The merchantman *Eliza*, commanded by Captain James Rowan, came to anchor in San Francisco Bay, the first American vessel to pass through the Golden Gate.

Sunday
25

1877—The first class of Revenue Cutter Service cadets began their training aboard the revenue cutter *J. C. Dobbin* at Curtis Bay, Maryland.

Merry are we, merry are we,
There's no one on earth like a sailor at sea.

—anon.

THE 19-FOOT YAWL *SILVER CLOUD*, NORTH SEA COAST OF ENGLAND, MAY 31, 1878

It was so calm that we only made Seaham, 5 miles south of Sunderland, by eight o'clock, when the tidal stream turned northward, and I found that to stay at sea was to be drifted back whence we came. Keeping the chart out of sight, I asked my little "mannie" where he thought the entrance was, and he pointed out a place which I knew was on the wrong side altogether of the harbour walls, but where they told us afterwards a yacht had three weeks ago landed, and in twelve hours gone to splinters, the three men in charge of her being saved; and all that remains of her now is the iron keel, which is offered for the very moderate sum of £1 sterling. Going forward to drop the anchor in the harbour here my mate had mistaken himself for the anchor, and plunged in instead. I thought the splash was unlike the wonted ring of the anchor, looked round, and, behold! shoulders above water, he was holding on by the small boat.

—William Forwell

PLUS ÇA CHANGE, PLUS C'EST LA MÊME CHOSE

Some young gentlemen when they get on board a yacht think it the correct thing to behave themselves in a way they would not dream of doing on shore. The fact of being afloat does not necessarily make one any the less a gentleman, and respectable people will not excuse any laxity in this respect, from the fact that the delinquent owns or is staying on board a yacht. Turning the saloon into a low class music hall, interlarding your conversation with objectionable adjectives, and scandalising a quiet port with bacchanalian orgies of the worst description, is certainly not the right way to enjoy that most manly of all sports, namely, Yachting.   —Tyrrel E. Biddle, 1881

The sooner [intellectuals] become aware that ships are manned by human beings and not by Hairy Apes the sooner we shall understand each other.
    —William McFee, marine engineer and novelist

We Durantes is cursed wid a love of the sea, and even now on a Saturday night will find me in my bath tub playin' wid my sailboat.
    —Jimmy Durante

What am I? A barnacle on the dinghy of life?
    —Popeye

*The true sailor is a born artist, a sportsman,
and above all a man of good instinct.*
                    —L. Francis Herreshoff

MAY/JUNE

Monday
26
MEMORIAL DAY / US
SPRING BANK HOLIDAY / UK

1703—Samuel Pepys, diarist and first secretary to the
British Admiralty, died in Clapham, England.

Tuesday
27

1936—Sally Stearns became the first female to compete in
a men's college varsity rowing team; as coxswain, she led
the Rollins College boat against Marietta College.

Wednesday
28

1967—Francis Chichester returned to Plymouth, England,
completing the first one-stop singlehanded circumnavigation
of the globe.

Thursday
29

1914—In the worst maritime disaster in Canadian history,
the passenger steamer *Empress of Ireland* collided with the
collier *Storstad* and sank in the St. Lawrence River; 1,024
lives were lost.

Friday
30

1995—The *Maria Assumpta*, 137 years old, at the time the
oldest large operational sailing vessel afloat, ran ashore near
Rumps Point, Cornwall, and was wrecked within minutes.

Saturday
31

1836—Francis Pettit Smith received a
patent for a screw propeller, which he
fitted to a 250-ton vessel, the *Archimedes*.

Sunday
1

1942—The first Loran-A navigational system pair
stations—Montauk Point, New York, and Fenwick
Island, Delaware—became permanently operational.

NAUTICAL EXPRESSIONS BASED ON THE WORD *WEATHER*

Weather—all things to windward

Weather beam—the side of a vessel facing the wind

Weather boards—boards along the rail, usually up forward, to block water and spray from coming aboard

Weather bound—held in port or at anchor because of foul weather

Weather cocking—heading bow-first into the wind

Weather eye, as in "Keep your weather eye open"—keep a good watch to windward

Weather gauge—the distance upwind of a vessel to another

Weather helm—the tendency of a vessel to turn up into the wind

Weather lurch—roll to windward

Weather shore—the shore to windward

Weather tide—a tidal current that pushes a vessel to windward

---

THE *BOUNTY*'S SHIP'S BOAT OFF THE EAST COAST OF NEW HOLLAND [AUSTRALIA], JUNE 4, 1789

Miserable as our situation was in every respect, I was secretly surprised to see that it did not appear to affect any one so strongly as myself; on the contrary, it seemed as if they had embarked on a voyage to Timor, in a vessel sufficiently calculated for safety and convenience. So much confidence gave me great pleasure, and I may assert that to this cause their preservation is chiefly to be attributed; for if any one of them had despaired, he would most probably have died before we reached New Holland. I now gave every one hopes that eight or ten days might bring us to a land of safety; and, after praying to God for a continuance of his most gracious protection, I served an allowance of water for supper, and kept my course to the WSW, to counteract the southerly winds, in case they should blow strong. We had been just six days on the coast of New Holland, in the course of which we found oysters, a few clams, some birds, and water.

—Lieutenant William Bligh, RN

*S*ailors are fond of adages.
—Anthony Bailey

FORETELLING THE WEATHER, A FEW OLD SAYINGS

Red sky in the morning,
Sailors take warning.

Sharp rise after blow
Foretells stronger blow.

Backing winds and mare's tails
Make tall ships carry low sails.

If the wind is northeast three days without rain,
Eight days will go by before south again.

If woolly fleeces deck the heavenly way
Be sure no rain will mar a summer's day.

Rain before seven
Clear by eleven.

When halo rings the moon or sun
Rain's approaching on the run.

Rainbow to windward: foul fall the day;
Rainbow to leeward: rain runs away.

Monday ○
2

1875—Construction began on jetties extending more than 2 miles to the seaward to improve navigation in the South Pass, where the Mississippi River enters the Gulf of Mexico.

Tuesday
3

1833—The *Ann McKim*, considered by many to be the first true clipper ship, was launched at Fells Point, Baltimore, Maryland.

Wednesday
4

1820—The first church established especially for mariners, founded by the New York Port Society, a nonsectarian, interdenominational religious organization, was opened in New York.

Thursday
5

1794—The U.S. Congress gave the Treasury Department administrative responsibility for lighthouses, beacons, buoys, and piers in navigable waters.

Friday
6

1650—Nicholas Lamius, a minister, saw a sea serpent crawl out of the sea on the coast of Norway.

Saturday
7

1881—John Pugh, fisherman of Westport, Nova Scotia, caught a large codfish whose stomach contained a splitting knife he had lost overboard a few days previously.

Sunday
8

1989—The wreck of the German battleship *Bismarck*, which had been sunk during World War II, was discovered approximately 600 miles west of Brest, France.

THE POWER OF SUPERSTITION, ACCORDING TO J. D. JERROLD KELLEY

In earlier days superstition was as much a part of every ship as the water she was to float in; for it entered with the wood scarfed into her keel, and climbed to the flags and garlands waving at her mast-heads; it ran riotously at her launching, controlled her name, her crew, and cargoes; it timed her days and hours of sailing, and convoyed her voyages. It summoned apparitions for her ill fortune, and evoked portents and signs for her prosperity; it made winds blow foul or fair, governed her successful ventures and arrivals, and, when her work was done, promised a port of rest somewhere off the shores of Fiddler's Green, where all good sailors rest eternally, or threatened foul moorings deep in the uncanny locker of Davy Jones of ballad memory.

BAD LUCK WILL FOLLOW IF

A hatch cover is left bottom up
An umbrella is brought on board
A black bag is brought on board
Church bells are heard while underway
A priest is allowed on board
A gull or an albatross or a porpoise is killed
    while underway
A shark follows the ship
The word *drown*, or *pig*, is spoken
A mop or bucket is lost overboard
A vessel is launched on a Friday
A voyage is begun on a Friday

A WATERFRONT LEGEND, OR SO THEY SAY

To dispel the old sailor's superstition that Friday was an unlucky day, verging on disastrous, a ship's keel was laid on a Friday, she was launched on a Friday, she was commissioned on a Friday, she was named *Friday*, her commander was Captain Friday, and she set sail on her maiden voyage on a Friday. She was neither seen nor heard from again. Or so they say.

THE PRIZE SLOOP *RANGER*, OFF THE COAST OF NOVA SCOTIA, JUNE 10–11, 1776

The 10th I was again in with Chebucto Head, and having struck soundings on a reef of rocks, in 8 fathom, I immediately let go the anchor, as the people as well as myself had taken no rest for forty-eight hours. Though from such a situation I had a right to expect the loss of both cable and anchor, yet I was fortunate enough to save them, and got under way at break of day in the morning, with a seeming prospect of getting soon into the harbour. But just as I was the length of Major's beach, and about to speak a Falmouth packet then coming down the river, she missed stays, which obliged me (being very near some dangerous rocks) to be quick in wearing; in consequence of which the boom came over, with the whole main sheet eased off, and carried it away in six different parts, which obliged me again to run from the narrow channel, and also lost me the satisfaction of speaking the packet.

—Bartholomew James

Monday ◑
9

2007—The Hawaiian canoe *Hokulea* arrived at Yokohama, Japan, following a five-month voyage of more than 8,500 miles across the Pacific Ocean.

Tuesday
10

1985—The *Rainbow Warrior*, manned by environmental activists, was sunk at her dock in Auckland, New Zealand, by what was believed to be members of the French secret service.

Wednesday
11

1788—Construction began at Nootka, British Columbia, on the schooner *Northwest America*, the first ship built by non-natives on the Pacific coast.

Thursday
12

1998—Eric Tabarly, winner of the 1964 singlehanded transatlantic race and several other ocean races after that, fell overboard and was lost in the Irish Sea.

Friday
13

1913—On a day that was thrice unlucky—a date with a thirteen in the day and the year—the square-rigger *Monkbarns* broached and was knocked down three times while running downwind in the Roaring Forties.

Saturday
14 FLAG DAY

1615—Willem Schouten of Hoorn set sail from the Netherlands on an expedition that would lend the name of his hometown to the southernmost tip of America—Cape Horn.

Sunday
15 FATHER'S DAY

1869—The light station at Cape Elizabeth, Maine, was fitted with a fog signal powered by a hot-air engine, the first in the United States.

THE 22-FOOT MOTOR LAUNCH *QUERIDA*, NEW YORK HARBOR, JUNE 19–20, 1907

About noon the fog dispersed. The sea was flat calm, the wind nil, while the thermometer soared and soared. Consequently we were all relieved when at 4:39 P.M. we tied up at 150th Street, North River, reaching port by the roundabout way of the Bronx Kills and the Harlem. The next day we lay off, that the crew might take in a few of Coney's roller coasters and Broadway roof-gardens, *Querida* merely running across the river and refilling her little 25-gallon copper tank. The run down the Sound had consumed approximately twenty gallons. Shortly before six on July 20th we crept tremblingly down the North River in a fog which thickened so among the ferries that we tied up for an hour on the Jersey side by the Erie slips. A little farther on we lost our bearings, then followed a tug bound for Perth Amboy. A severe thunderstorm struck us in the Kills, but the sun came out when we were running up the Raritan trying to follow the channel without running into our ensign. The sparkling, limpid waters of the canal received us, and at Bound Brooks we tied up for the night near the auxiliary yawl *Cricket*, of Bridgeport, Connecticut.

—"Her Captain"

SUGGESTED PROVISIONS FOR A LONG VOYAGE, 17ᵀᴴ CENTURY, ACCORDING TO CAPTAIN JOHN SMITH

Fine Wheat Flower close and well packed, Rice, Currands, Sugar, Prunes, Cynamon, Ginger, Pepper, Clover, Oyle, Butter, Holland Cheese, Wine Vinegar, Canarie Sacke, Agua Vitae [brandy], the best Wines, the best Waters, the juyce of limons for the Scurvy, White Bisket, Oatmeale, Gammons of Bacon, dried Neates tongues, Beef packed up in Vinegar, Legs of Mutton minced and stewed and close packed up with tried sewet or butter in earthern pots.

L. FRANCIS HERRESHOFF, YACHT DESIGNER AND GASTRONOMIST, ON EATING

Take my advice—eat your potatoes with their jackets on; eat your whole apple, skin, core, and all; chew everything well. Don't forget the prunes.

SAILORS' BEEF AND PORK IS VERY SCANT,
I'm sure of weight one half it want;
A kind of horse beans they do get for pease,
No nourishment at all there is in these;
Instead of English cheese or butter
A little oyl we get, God wot, far worser.
A little rice we get instead of fish
Which unto you is known, but a poor dish:
Except good sauce to put it in you had,
For with good sauce a deal-board is not bad.
—from a 17th-century naval ballad

The cook is the seagoing equivalent of the mother-in-law. He is the perpetual butt of the shellback's ridicule or abuse.
—C. Fox Smith

We should all be the fitter, the happier and better if we could return to the wide horizons of land and sea.

                                                —Basil Lubbock

JUNE

Monday
16

1987—Following her restoration, HMS *Warrior*, the first iron battle-ship and the most powerful warship of her time when launched in 1860, returned to Portsmouth, England, for exhibition.

Tuesday
17

1851—The clipper ship *Staffordshire*, designed and built by Donald McKay, was launched in East Boston, Massachusetts.

Wednesday
18

1878—An Act of Congress created the U.S. Lifesaving Service as a distinct entity under the Treasury Department.

Thursday
19

1876—The first U.S. Lifesaving Medal was awarded to Lucian M. Clemons, keeper of the U.S. Lifesaving Service Station, Marble-head, Ohio, for valor in saving the crew of the schooner *Consuelo*.

Friday
20

1945—The USS *Sanctuary*, a hospital ship, the first ship in the U.S. Navy with a mixed company of male and female personnel, was commissioned.

Saturday
21 SUMMER SOLSTICE

1919—The crews of the captured German battle fleet interned in Scapa Flow, Orkney Islands, scuttled their ships; a total of 52 vessels—battleships, battle cruisers, light cruisers, and destroyers—went to the bottom.

Sunday
22

1877—The revolutionary catamaran *Amaryllis*, designed and built by Nathanael G. Herreshoff, while sailing at great speed in a match race, drove her bows under and pitchpoled.

GMT (GREENWICH MEAN TIME) IS NOW KNOWN AS UTC (UNIVERSAL TIME COORDINATED)

UTC uses the 0-degree meridian of longitude running through the observatory at Greenwich, England, as its benchmark.

UTC minus 4 hours = Atlantic Standard Time
UTC minus 5 hours = Eastern Standard Time
UTC minus 6 hours = Central Standard Time
etc.

THE RACING KETCH *ANEMONE*, PACIFIC OCEAN NEAR THE HAWAIIAN ISLANDS, JUNE 25, 1906

We are looking for land now, and the Captain thinks he can see "the loom" of it. We landlubbers can't see anything but a cloudbank. Last night we saw a startling cloud effect which moved even the stolid captain to expressive admiration. On the edge of a large dark cloudbank appeared in snowy white a perfect image of a lady in evening dress—with a large fur mantle over her shoulders. As the picture was gradually diffused, the lady became old. Finally it represented an old ragamuffin hobbling on a crutch. The picture was at all times so strikingly real that we all agreed in our interpretation. This morning at five we had land in sight, the Island of Molokai, on the port bow. The captain has certainly done good navigating: we are off the channel between the Islands Molokai and Oahu, just where we want to be. A good breeze is blowing and we ought to reach Diamond Head, on Oahu, by noon.

—Louis A. E. Ahlers

AT SEA, THE 24-HOUR DAY IS DIVIDED INTO SEVEN WATCHES

Mid watch—midnight to 4 a.m. (0000–0400)
Morning watch—4 a.m. to 8 a.m. (0400–0800)
Forenoon watch—8 a.m. to noon (0800–1200)
Afternoon watch—noon to 4 p.m. (1200–1600)
First dog watch—4 p.m. to 6 p.m. (1600–1800)
Second dog watch—6 p.m. to 8 p.m. (1800–2000)
Evening watch, aka first watch—8 p.m. to midnight (2000–2400)

TIME SLANG, U.S. NAVY

"Midbitch," "Midshitter," "The Churchyard," "Balls to Four"—the mid watch, from midnight to 4 a.m.
"Four-by-Eight," "The Deadeye"—the morning watch, 4 a.m. to 8 a.m.
"Oh-Dark-Thirty," "Zero-Dark-Thirty"—late at night, or early in the morning
"Bell Tapper"—anyone who is always late, especially when relieving the watch

The ship's clock in the bar says half past eleven. Half past eleven is opening time. The hands of the clock have stayed still at half past eleven for fifty years. It is always opening time in the Sailor's Arms.

—from *Under Milk Wood*, by Dylan Thomas

There are three sorts of people: those who are alive,
those who are dead, and those who are at sea.
                                                    —anon.

JUNE

Monday
23

1904—The first organized motorboat race in the
United States, sponsored by the Columbia Yacht Club,
got underway on the Hudson River, New York.

Tuesday
24

1904—The 59-foot launch *Standard*, 100 hp, driven by
C. C. Riotte, won the first organized motorboat race with
an average speed of 19.67 knots.

Wednesday
25

1916—Artist Thomas Eakins, painter of *The Pair-Oared
Shell* and other works with a rowing theme, died in
Philadelphia, Pennsylvania.

Thursday
26

1976—Tim Severin with a crew of four reached Newfoundland
after crossing the North Atlantic from Ireland in the oxhide
coracle *Brendan*, to prove that St. Brendan could have made
the passage in ancient times.

Friday
27

1875—A sailor gone mad on the clipper ship *Jessie Osborne*
who had been 5 days aloft with a chisel, progressively cutting
away the rigging, out of reach of the deck gang, was shot
dead by a sharpshooter.

Saturday
28

1815—A U.S. fleet commanded by Commodore Stephen
Decatur entered the Bay of Algiers and, under the threat
of destruction of the port, dictated a peace with Algiers.

Sunday
29

WHOOPIE PIE DAY

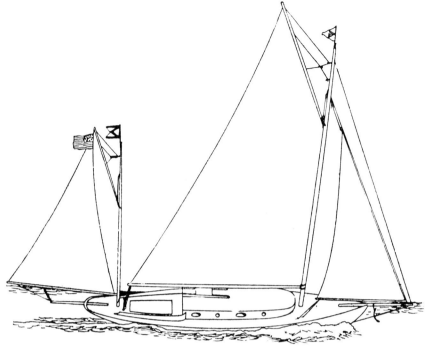

It is a well-known fact that the oftener one goes cruising, the fewer unnecessaries are taken.
—Dixon Kemp

HOW TO SPOT A REAL CRUISING BOAT, ACCORDING TO WINTHROP P. MOORE

A cruising boat usually gives herself away at a glance because of the special gear which is in evidence. On sailing yachts the rigging of the lines and stays will indicate at once to the experienced boatman that she is intended for open water use. There will be chafing gear (called baggywrinkle) in the shrouds and on the spreaders, which is designed to prevent or minimize chafe on the sails. There will be special provision for ventilation, because frequently it is impossible to run with the skylights and hatches open. And, above all, there will be a minimum of gear about the decks to impede progress when sail making is in order.

SIMPLIFY, SIMPLIFY, SAYS JEROME K. JEROME

Throw the lumber over, man! Let your boat of life be light, packed with only what you need —a homely home and simple pleasures, one or two friends, worth the name, someone to love and someone to love you, a cat, a dog, and a pipe or two, enough to eat and enough to wear, and a little more than enough to drink; for thirst is a dangerous thing.

In this world it seems that the less things we need, the happier we are; then everything but the bare necessities becomes a luxury and fills us with content.
—Uffa Fox

THE MAIL STEAMER *VIRGINIA LAKE,* COAST OF LABRADOR, JULY 4, 1906

We saw for the first time the bleak, rock-bound coast of Labrador. In all the earth there is no coast so barren, so desolate, so brutally inhospitable as the Labrador coast from Cape Charles, at the Strait of Belle Isle on the south, to Cape Chidley on the north.... It is a fog-ridden, dangerous coast, with never a lighthouse or signal of any kind at any point in its entire length to warn or guide the mariner. The evening was well upon us when we saw the rocks off Cape Charles rising from the water, dismal, and dark, and forbidding. All day the rain had been falling, and all day the wind had been blowing a gale, lashing the sea into a fury. Our little ship was tossed about like a cork, with the seas constantly breaking over her decks. Decidedly our introduction to Labrador was not auspicious. Battle Harbour, twelve miles north of Cape Charles, was to have been our first stop; but there are treacherous hidden reefs at the entrance, and with that sea the captain did not care to trust his ship near them. So he ran on to Spear Harbour, just beyond, where we lay to for the night.
—Dillon Wallace

In gallant trim the gilded vessel goes;
Youth on the prow, and Pleasure at the helm.
—Thomas Gray

JUNE/JULY

Monday
30

1848—Edward Burgess, yacht designer, was born in Sandwich, Cape Cod, Massachusetts.

Tuesday ○
1

1881—*Valkyr*, the first of the so-called compromise cutters, a combination of the best attributes of the British cutter and the American centerboard sloop, designed by A. Cary Smith, was launched in New York.

Wednesday
2

1878—The Hudson River sloop *Illinois*, built in 1818 and one of the earliest of her type, was run down and sunk by a steamer in Long Island Sound; she was later raised and continued her career until 1893.

Thursday
3

1927—Ensign Charles L. Duke, commander of a U.S. Coast Guard patrol boat, boarded the rumrunner *Greypoint* in New York Harbor and singlehandedly captured the 22-man crew and its cargo of illegal liquor.

Friday
4 INDEPENDENCE DAY

1928—Jean Lussier became the first daredevil to go over Niagara Falls in a rubber ball and survive.

Saturday
5

1946—On a banner day for rubberneckers, the bikini bathing suit was introduced by designer Louis Réard at a fashion show in Paris, France.

Sunday
6

1747—John Paul Jones, naval hero of the American Revolution, was born in Arbigland, Kirkbean, Kirkcudbright, Scotland.

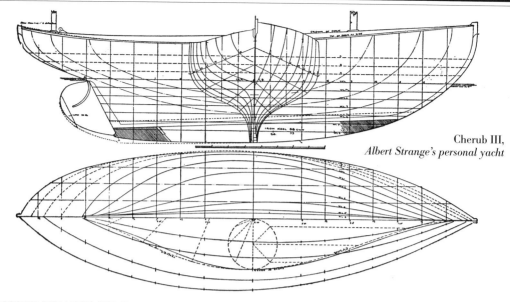

Cherub III,
Albert Strange's personal yacht

ALBERT STRANGE AND THE DEVELOPMENT OF THE POCKET CRUISER

Albert Strange (1855–1917) was a professional artist, a sailor, a writer, and a yacht designer specializing in small craft, particularly canoe-yawls. The canoe-yawl had its roots in the decked canoe, the evolution of which in the late nineteenth century branched off in three directions: the paddling-only, the paddling-and-sailing, and the pure-sailing types. Albert Strange and other English designers and sailors quickly took the lead in the development of the latter craft, starting with the modification of the Rob Roy decked canoe with a larger sail rig and ending several decades later with the so-called canoe-yawl—a small sailboat suggestive of the pocket cruiser of today whose only resemblance to a canoe was a double-ended hull. Albert Strange did much to help popularize the type. He wrote and illustrated several stories about his canoe-yawl cruises that were published in yachting magazines of the day, and also wrote a valuable series on the practical aspects of yacht design that was published from 1914–15 in Britain's *Yachting Monthly* magazine.

WHY SMALL BOATS CAN TAKE BIG SEAS, ACCORDING TO WINTHROP P. MOORE

Small boats, offering less obstruction to the action of the waves because of their buoyancy, will float along on the top of everything, while great steamers are hammering into the waves and suffering damage. Another important factor is the difference in wave lengths. During a storm the distance from crest to crest of waves may be several hundred feet. This means that the small boat will never straddle waves, nor will she plunge into the trough at the same time that her stern is being pushed up by the passing wave. In other words, a small boat will ride on top of big waves, taking no green water aboard, when a larger vessel is finding the going extremely uncomfortable and must slow down for safety.

A PACKET SHIP TO LISBON, ENGLISH CHANNEL, JULY 11, 1754

A most tragical incident fell out this day at sea. While the ship was under sail, but making as will appear no great way, a kitten, one of four of the feline inhabitants of the cabin, fell from the window into the water: an alarm was immediately given to the captain, who was then upon deck, and received it with the utmost concern and many bitter oaths. He immediately gave orders to the steersman in favor of the poor thing, as he called it; the sails were instantly slackened, and all hands, as the phrase is, employed to recover the poor animal. I was, I own, extremely surprised at all this; less indeed at the captain's extreme tenderness than at his conceiving any possibility of success; for if puss had had nine thousand instead of nine lives, I concluded they had been all lost. The boatswain, however, had more sanguine hopes, for, having stripped himself of his jacket, breeches, and shirt, he leaped boldly into the water, and to my great astonishment in a few minutes returned to the ship, bearing the motionless animal in his mouth.

—Henry Fielding

The smaller the vessel, the better the sport.

—anon.

JULY

Monday
7

1951—L. G. Van de Wiele departed Nice, France, in the 45-foot ketch *Omoo* on a circumnavigation of the globe for which he would be awarded the Blue Water Medal of the Cruising Club of America.

Tuesday ◐
8

1999—Ken-ichi Horie arrived in Japan after a 102-day transpacific voyage from San Francisco in the junk-rigged sailboat *Malt's Mermaid II*, built of welded-together beer kegs.

Wednesday
9

1825—The four-oared racing gig *American Star* was presented by the citizens of the United States to General Lafayette of France, who was visiting New York, in appreciation for his assistance during the American Revolution.

Thursday
10

1899—The schooner-yacht *Cambria*, America's Cup challenger and winner of a famous transatlantic race with the *Dauntless*, was broken up for scrap.

Friday
11

1917—Albert Strange, yacht designer, best known for his canoe yawls, died in England.

Saturday
12

1836—Charles Haynes Haswell, the first officer in the U.S. Navy to be assigned as an engineer, was promoted to chief engineer.

Sunday
13

1836—John Ericsson, who had emigrated from Sweden to England, was awarded a British patent for a screw propeller.

A SEAWORTHY OPEN BOAT

The Bank dory, the classic North American small-boat type, got its name from the location of its principal use—the Grand Bank off Newfoundland. It is an open boat used in the fisheries for setting trawl lines. It has a tombstone transom, raking stem with a slight curvature, flat, narrow bottom with little rocker, high freeboard, flared sides, and strong sheer. In the old Bank fishery, it was propelled by oars in tholepins, with auxiliary sail. It has a longitudinally planked bottom with no keel structure, widely spaced sawn frames, and lapped side planking. Most are built with removable thwarts so they can be "nested," one inside another.

THOREAU'S RIVER BOAT WAS A DORY

Our boat, which had cost us a week's labor in the spring, was in form like a fisherman's dory, fifteen feet long by three and a half in breadth at the widest part, painted green below, with a border of blue, with reference to the two elements in which it was to spend its existence. It had been loaded the evening before at our door, half a mile from the river, with potatoes and melons from a patch which we had cultivated, and a few utensils; and was provided with wheels in order to be rolled around falls, as well as with two sets of oars, and several slender poles for shoving in shallow places, and also two masts, one of which served for a tent pole at night; for a buffalo skin was to be our bed, and a tent of cotton cloth our roof. It was strongly built, but heavy, and hardly of better model than usual.

—from *A Week on the Concord and Merrimack Rivers*, by Henry David Thoreau

PHILIP C. BOLGER, YACHT DESIGNER, ON ADMISSION TO HEAVEN

When I come up for judgment and they stop me at the gate and ask, "What's your excuse?" I'll tell them I designed the Gloucester Light Dory and they'll have to let me in.

THE 19-FOOT DORY *NAUTILUS*, ATLANTIC OCEAN, JULY 16, 1878

Wind E. and variable; very light. Saw five sails going to westward. Get some wind in afternoon, but it shifts frequently, blowing in strong gusts. At midnight saw green light and shadow approaching off the starboard bow. Showed my light (which I keep under the seat now for two reasons—viz., we get the heat from it and can see more distinctly), and bore down on him, but he bore away from me, taking me for a steamer or a nondescript; but I gave chase, and getting over their scare, they hove to. I ran alongside and explained things. She proved to be the Norwegian barque *Franc*, Captain Petersen. The captain…had to rub his eyes a long time before he would believe that he was awake, and that we were really a legitimate Yankee craft. Wanted us to come on board, but we declined, and bid him good-bye.

—William A. Andrews

Monday
14

1841—Elimination heats in a U.S. rowing race were held for the first time, at a regatta on the Hudson River in Newburgh, New York.

Tuesday
15

1941—Robert Neilson arrived in San Pedro, California, in the 30-foot ketch *Orion* at the end of a passage from Honolulu, Hawaii, for which he would be awarded the Blue Water Medal of the Cruising Club of America.

Wednesday
16

1912—The motorboat *Detroit*, skippered by Thomas Fleming Day, editor of *The Rudder* magazine, departed Vineyard Haven, Massachusetts, on a transatlantic run to Queenstown (now Cobh), Ireland.

Thursday
17

1761—The 29-mile-long Bridgewater Canal, the first great inland canal to be dug in England, opened for commercial traffic.

Friday
18

1892—Thomas Cook, who made his fortune booking travel excursions, most by steamship and railroad, died in Leicester, England.

Saturday
19

1917—*Miss Minneapolis*, a Gold Cup race boat, became the first motorboat to break the mile-a-minute barrier in an official race, achieving 65.7 miles per hour at Put-in-Bay, Ohio.

Sunday
20

1813—The island of Bermuda was struck by a major hurricane that destroyed approximately one-third of the houses and drove most of the shipping ashore.

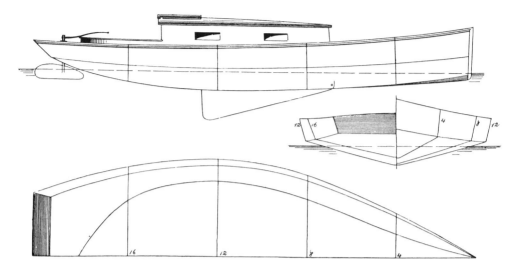

COLIN ARCHER

Colin Archer (1832–1921), a Norwegian born of Scottish parents, designed and built ships, boats, and yachts that reflected Scandinavian character—that is, strong, seaworthy, and capable vessels. His most famous ship built in his yard in Larvik, Norway, was the *Fram*, an auxiliary steam schooner first used by Fridtjof Nansen for Arctic exploration and later by Roald Amundsen for his Antarctic expedition to reach the South Pole. Archer's enduring legacy is a series of fifty-two ketch-rigged sailing redningsskoites (rescue boats) for the Norsk Selskad til Skibrudnes Redning, the Norwegian Society for the Rescue of the Ship-wrecked. Many of these craft were later converted to yachts when they were no longer needed for lifesaving. While not exactly speedsters, their ability to go anywhere, under any circumstance, made them the perfect workhorses for offshore cruising. Many twentieth-century sailors made their fame in yachts either designed by Archer or inspired by him: Vito Dumas in *Lehg II*, Robin Knox-Johnston in *Suhaili*, Erskine Childers in *Aasgard*, William Nutting in *Leiv Eiriksson*, and Rockwell Kent in *Direction*.

LAYING OUT A YACHT DESIGN ON A SHEET OF PAPER, GENERAL CONVENTIONS

Profile, top left; plan view, bottom left; body plan, top right; legend, bottom right.

Stern to the left, bow to the right.

Stations marked off from right to left—i.e., station 0 will be forward.

Body plan drawn with half-sections for each station; forebody half-sections to the right of the centerline, afterbody half-sections to the left.

WEIGHT EQUALS MUSCLE, SAYS E. F. KNIGHT

The general requirements in a yacht are speed, accommodation, sail-carrying power, and weight. This latter property means, in other words, the ability to drive through a sea that, from its wall-sidedness, makes it an impractical barrier to get over. When a vessel has not the weight or power to meet such a sea, as a rule, it spells disaster, or, to say the least, very disagreeable consequences.

THE U.S. BRIG *ARGUS*, ENGLISH CHANNEL, JULY 24–27, 1813

July 24. Captured this morning a large brig from Madeira for England laden with wine, got a few ½ pipes of the best on board intended for the use of the Countess of Shaftesbury—£8.800 sterling—Stove nearly all the rest.

July 25. Saw a fleet of 11 sail this morning a frigate among them—also a large sail to windward—spoke her—she proved a polacre ship from Lisbon to London Portuguese—fleet out of sight.

July 26. Mouth of the Channel. Discovered a Square rigged vessell this morning—from her appearance supposed an American Standing before the wind up Channell—Did not give chace as it would carry us too far up the channell—especially as the wind is from the Westward.

July 27. Captured a large English Brig the Richard from Giberalter in ballast. Took out the Capt & Crew and a female Passenger & burnt her.   —Surgeon James Inderwick

Monday
21

1960−Francis Chichester won the first singlehanded
transatlantic yacht race, from England to North America.

Tuesday
22

1832−Colin Archer, designer of the Norwegian redningsskoites (rescue boats) on which so many cruising boats have
been based, was born at Tolderodden, Larvik, Norway.

Wednesday
23

1887−Joshua Slocum, the first person to sail alone around
the world, while captain of the bark *Aquidneck* killed one
man and wounded another in Antonina, Brazil; he was
acquitted at trial after pleading self-defense.

Thursday ◖
24

1998−Canada Post issued a commemorative stamp bearing
the image of W. J. Roué, designer of the legendary racing
fishing schooner *Bluenose*.

Friday
25

1902−Eric Hoffer−longshoreman, philosopher, author−was
born in the Bronx, New York.

Saturday
26

1786−A "skiff-steamboat," designed and built by John
Fitch, made a trial run at Philadelphia, Pennsylvania.

Sunday
27

1996−The cruise ship *Universe Explorer*
caught fire in Alaska's Inside Passage; 5 in the
crew died, 76 people on board were injured.

TACKING SHIP OFF SHORE
by Walter Mitchell

The weather-leech of the topsail shivers,
The bowlines strain, and the lee-shrouds slacken,
The braces are taut, the lithe boom quivers,
And the waves with the coming squall-cloud
    blacken.

Open one point on the weather-bow,
Is the lighthouse tall on Fire Island Head.
There's a shade of doubt on the captain's brow,
And the pilot watches the heaving lead.

I stand at the wheel, and with eager eye
To sea and to sky and to shore I gaze,
Till the muttered order of "Full and by!"
Is suddenly changed for "Full for stays!"

The ship bends lower before the breeze,
As her broadside fair to the blast she lays;
And she swifter springs to the rising seas,
As the pilot calls, "Stand by for stays!"

It is silence all, as each in his place,
With the gathered coil in his hardened hands,
By tack and bowline, by sheet and brace,
Waiting the watchword impatient stands.

And the light on Fire Island Head draws near,
As, trumpet-winged, the pilot's shout
From his post on the bowsprit's heel I hear,
With the welcome call of "Ready! About!"

No time to spare! It is touch and go;
And the captain growls, "Down helm! hard down!"
As my weight on the whirling spokes I throw,
While heaven grows black with the storm-cloud's
    frown.

High o'er the knight-heads flies the spray,
As we meet the shock of the plunging sea;
And my shoulder stiff to the wheel I lay,
As I answer, "Ay, ay, sir! Ha-a-rd a-lee!"

With the swerving leap of a startled steed
The ship flies fast in the eye of the wind,
The dangerous shoals on the lee recede,
And the headland white we have left behind.

The topsails flutter, the jibs collapse,
And belly and tug at the groaning cleats;
The spanker slats, and the mainsail flaps;
And thunders the order, "Tacks and sheets!"

Mid the rattle of blocks and the tramp of the
    crew,
Hisses the rain of the rushing squall:
The sails are aback from clew to clew,
And now is the moment for "Mainsail, haul!"

And the heavy yards, like a baby's toy,
By fifty strong arms are swiftly swung:
She holds her way, and I look with joy
For the first white spray o'er the bulwarks flung.

"Let go, and haul!" 'Tis the last command,
And the head-sails fill to the blast once more:
Astern and to leeward lies the land,
With its breakers white on the shingly shore.

What matters the reef, or the rain, or the squall?
I steady the helm for the open sea;
The first mate clamors, "Belay, there, all!"
And the captain's breath once more comes free.

And so off shore let the good ship fly;
Little care I how the gusts may blow,
In my fo'castle bunk, in a jacket dry.
Eight bells have struck, and my watch is below.

THE YAWL *ALGA*, LONG ISLAND SOUND, AUGUST 2, 1902

The breeze freshened until our lee rail was awash, and with a calm sea we sped toward Saybrook, just visible in the haze.... The wind stayed with us all the way, although the water to the East was as calm as a sea of glass. We dropped the mainsail as we stood up between the jetties at the mouth of the Connecticut. The knockabout *Lorna*, of New Haven, lay in the river off the Hartford Y. C. and we rounded to at a good distance to the North of her, but to our amazement had to drop anchor hastily to avoid fouling her. We had not figured on the strong ebb-tide. The Skipper took out the light anchor to kedge up to a safe distance, but for some reason unknown (it was carefully dropped) it came right in, fouling the hawse of both yachts. With *Lorna*'s help we got everything clear and a Hartford Y. C. auxiliary towed us to a better anchorage.

—F. Atwater Ward

Monday
28

1869—The floating drydock *Bermuda*, at the time the largest floating structure in the world, arrived at Bermuda under tow from England.

Tuesday
29

1865—The first issue of the *Atlantic Telegraph*, the first newspaper to be published at sea, was distributed aboard the cable-laying ship *Great Eastern*.

Wednesday
30

1865—In the worst maritime disaster to date on the West Coast, the sidewheel passenger steamer *Brother Jonathan* struck a rock off Point St. George, California, and sank, with the loss of 225 lives.

Thursday ○
31

1890—George L. Schuyler, the last survivor of the original schooner-yacht *America* syndicate, died aboard Elbridge T. Gerry's steam yacht *Electra* in New London Harbor, Connecticut.

Friday
1

1819—Herman Melville, author of *Moby-Dick*, *White Jacket*, and other novels of the sea, was born in New York City.

Saturday
2

1973—The French bathyscaph *Archimede* made the first manned dive into the Mid-Atlantic Rift, an underwater valley that runs along the Mid-Atlantic Ridge.

Sunday
3

1816—Ferdinand Rudolph Hassler was appointed the first superintendent of the U.S. Coast Survey, the principal task of which was to survey the coast for the preparation of navigational charts.

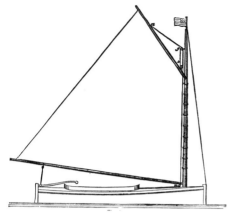

CAPE COD–STYLE CATBOAT

A wide, shallow, centerboard sailing boat common to Cape Cod, though its origins are in New York. Known in Britain as a una boat. Originally used by inshore fishermen, it was adapted for pleasure use in the late nineteenth, early twentieth centuries. The major characteristics are a huge gaff-rigged mainsail (though some of the racing cats were fitted with a bowsprit and a jib); a stubby, stout mast; a barn-door rudder; a large, heavy centerboard; and a high bow. The typical cruising catboat is decked over with the forward half of the hull given over to a house and the after half to a large cockpit. The length on deck varies from as small as 10 feet to as much as 35 feet.

A 20-FOOT CRUISING CATBOAT, NEWPORT, RHODE ISLAND, AUGUST 10, 1906

About one o'clock in the morning the Mate was aroused by some one calling. Crawling out of the cabin, he saw the Captain rowing as hard as he could in our little nine-foot tender, and asking piteously where he was and what he was doing. The Captain had gotten up in his sleep, stepped into the tender, cast her loose and rowed ashore and, half-way back, on waking up was very much frightened at finding himself adrift in that small craft. We sailed at 4:35 in a thick fog for New London.... Point Judith Breakwater was as much as we could make that day, so we ran in there to spend the night. I rowed over to a lobsterman to buy some lobsters for supper. On asking him how much he would charge for five or six of them, he said he would sell a whole keg of them for fifty cents; but I said that I only needed a few, so he threw a dozen of them into my boat, and I rowed back and we had a very good supper of lobsters and coffee.

—Pearce P. Williams

A single sail does not necessarily denote simplicity in handling.
—Carl Lane

ADVANTAGES OF A CENTERBOARD BOAT

Able to sail in thin water and moor in anchorages unsuitable for deep-draft craft.

Will generally remain upright when aground, or close to it.

Relatively easy to load on a trailer.

Hauling up the board reduces underwater friction in a broad reach and a run.

Steering trim can be adjusted by the incremental raising and lowering of the board.

In shoal water, the board scraping on the bottom acts as a built-in sounding device.

A board on a pin will reduce the effects of going hard aground by absorbing much of the shock.

DISADVANTAGES OF A CENTERBOARD BOAT

Added construction and maintenance expense.

The trunk can—and eventually will—leak.

In a daysailer, the trunk takes up leg room; in a cruising boat, it takes up living space.

The board can jam in the trunk; given Murphy's Law, it will happen at a time when such is least expected or desired.

Self-righting ability is either nonexistent or impaired.

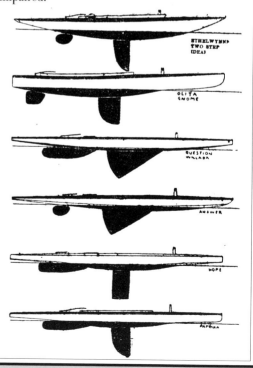

AUGUST

Monday
4

1806—London's East India Docks, constructed specially to serve ships in the East Indian trade, were opened for business.

Tuesday
5

1918—SS *Quistconck*, the first of the "Hog Islanders"—emergency merchant ships built during World War I—was launched at the Hog Island Shipyard, Philadelphia.

Wednesday
6

1983—A fire aboard the *Castillo de Bellver* off Cape Town, South Africa, caused a major spill of 250,000 tons of oil.

Thursday
7

1789—An Act of Congress was passed "for the establishment and support of lighthouses, beacons, buoys and public piers."

Friday
8

1886—Two men in a watertight cask passed safely through the Whirlpool Rapids, Niagara Falls, New York.

Saturday
9

1950—Congress passed an act assigning the U.S. Coast Guard the responsibility for maintaining port security in the United States.

Sunday
10

1856—A hurricane-driven tidal surge swept over Low Island, Louisiana; approximately 140 lives were lost.

DEVELOPMENT OF THE AUDIO FOG SIGNAL
Bell—early times
Trumpet—mid-17th century
Cannon—early 18th century
Steam whistle—mid-19th century
Hot-air whistle—mid-19th century
Siren—mid-19th century
Submarine bell—early 20th century
Compressed-air horn—early 20th century
Electrically powered diaphragm—
mid-20th century

FOG TERMS USED BY NOAA, THE NATIONAL OCEANIC AND ATMOSPHERIC ADMINISTRATION

Advection fog—a type of fog that results from the advection of moist air over a cold surface and the cooling of the air to its dew point that follows; this type of fog is most common in coastal regions.

Dense fog—a fog in which visibility is less than one-quarter mile.

Fog—water that has condensed close to ground level, producing a cloud of very small droplets that reduces visibility to less than 3,300 feet.

Fogbow—a rainbow that has a white band that appears in fog, and is fringed with red on the outside and blue on the inside.

Ground fog—shallow fog (less than 20 feet deep) produced over the land by the cooling of the lower atmosphere as it comes in contact with the ground. Also known as radiation fog.

Ice fog—a suspension of numerous minute ice crystals in the air, or water droplets at temperatures below 0° Celsius, based at the Earth's surface, which reduces horizontal visibility. Usually occurs at −20°F and below. Also called freezing fog.

Mist—consists of microscopic water droplets suspended in the air that produce a thin, grayish veil over the landscape. It reduces visibility to a lesser extent than fog.

Overrunning—a condition that exists when a relatively warm air mass moves up and over a colder and denser air mass on the surface. The result is usually low clouds, fog, and steady, light precipitation.

Shallow fog—fog in which the visibility at 6 feet above ground level is 5/8 of a mile or more.

Steam fog (also known as sea smoke)—fog that is formed when water vapor is added to air that is much colder than the vapor's source. This is most common when very cold air drifts across relatively warm water.

THE CENTERBOARD SCHOONER *CHAMPLAIN*, ST. LAWRENCE RIVER NEAR QUEBEC CITY, AUGUST 12, 1887

The tide was with us, but the breeze was light as we sailed down the river past the Falls of Montmorency, a sheet of water that thundered down into the St. Lawrence over a cliff two hundred feet high. We coasted along the wooded margin of the Isle Orleans for twenty miles. The wind died out to a mere breath, and we floated with the tide at the rate of four knots an hour.... In 10 minutes we were in a fog, the thickest I ever saw. You could actually fill your mouth with it and chew it. You don't credit that, you say; well, it is a fact but I'll give you further proof of its density. During a squall all my fresh water was spilled, and I could not use the river water to make coffee, owing to its brackishness. I just went on deck, took a few handfuls of the fog and packed it down tightly in the coffee pot, and you could not ask for better coffee than I made with it.

—J. Armoy Knox

Monday
11

<small>PLAY-IN-THE-SAND DAY</small>

Tuesday
12

1947—Bowdoin B. Crowninshield, naval architect, designer of the America's Cup contender *Independence* and the seven-masted schooner *Thomas W. Lawson*, died in Marblehead, Massachusetts.

Wednesday
13

1912—The U.S. Congress passed an Act to Regulate Radio Communications, which required all operators and stations, including those aboard ships at sea, to be licensed.

Thursday
14

1834—The brig *Pilgrim* with Richard Henry Dana Jr. aboard, set sail on a voyage from Boston, Massachusetts, around Cape Horn, to California.

Friday
15

1954—Water-skier Warren Witherell jumped 106 feet on Lake Winnipesaukee, New Hampshire, the first to jump more than 100 feet on water skis.

Saturday
16

1829—The packet ship *Sachem* docked in Boston, Massachusetts; on board were the original Siamese twins, Chang and Eng Bunker.

Sunday
17

This day marks the Roman festival of Portunus, the god of doors, gates, and harbors.

THE PRINCIPAL MIND-SET OF THE SINGLE-HANDER, ACCORDING TO CHARLES PEARS

There are many qualities that go to make the singlehander. First of all, let those who would understand him remember that his cruises are not regarded by him in the light of outings; they border more upon the scientific. Each cruise is an experiment, and, as it is impossible to get two minds to work as one, he becomes a singlehander. He prefers to be thought of as an amateur sailor; to him the term yachtsman implies a glorified beanfeaster.

THE SINGLEHANDED LUGGER *PROCYON*, ENGLISH CHANNEL, AUGUST 20, 1878

I had taken a little burnt brandy and biscuit at intervals, by the time the Foreland was rounded, and Deal in sight, I felt there was a terrible void within, and for the first time since leaving Greenhithe began to anticipate the pleasure of a substantial breakfast, which the adverse tide and long distance to be run before she could be hove-to was certain to postpone to a very late hour.... After luffing out of the rough sea into the comparatively smooth water of Margate Roads, the yard was lowered as for reefing, the upper tack-tackle bowsed down to two blocks, and the main sheet hauled flat aft from the fourth cringle with the reef tackle, which completed the operation, and was equivalent to putting her temporarily under four reefs.... When this was done, and the lugger was standing up for the roads with no more demand upon my services than occasional supervision and correction, I threw off waterproofs, and I fear indulged in an unseeming exhibition of hilarity.

—R. T. McMullen

ACCORDING TO C. P. KUNHARDT, A SINGLEHANDER'S YACHT MUST BE

As small as possible for size of the sailor
Safe—not probably, but absolutely
Easy to control
Fitted with permanent accommodations
Seaworthy and able
Handsome and smart, with an attractive finish

THE EARLY YEARS OF THE SAILING SINGLEHANDER, THE SO-CALLED POOR MAN'S YACHT

1865—Captain John MacGregor introduced the first Rob Roy canoe, based on the ancient Eskimo kayak.

1867—MacGregor took delivery of the 21-foot yawl *Rob Roy*, the first of the singlehanders to be designed as such.

1868—MacGregor's book *The Voyage Alone in the Yawl Rob Roy* was published.

1869—E. E. Middleton, inspired by *The Voyage Alone*, circumnavigated the British Isles in the 21-foot cutter *Kate*.

1869—Warrington Baden-Powell and a friend, each in his own Rob Roy canoe, cruised the waterways of Denmark and Sweden.

1871—Warrington Baden-Powell published his book *Canoe Travelling*.

Monday
18

1926—The yawl *Ilex* won the second Fastnet Race, from the Isle of Wight, England, to Fastnet Rock, Ireland, and finishing in Plymouth, England.

Tuesday
19

1866—The metal lifeboat *Red, White, and Blue* sailed up the River Thames to London, England, at the end of a transatlantic voyage from New York.

Wednesday
20

1933—Ralph Middleton Munroe, yacht designer well known for his shoal-draft craft, died in Coconut Grove, Florida.

Thursday
21

1918—The Gloucester fishing schooners *A.P. Andrew* and *Francis J. O'Hara Jr.* and the Canadian schooner *Una A. Saunders* were boarded by a crew from the German submarine *U-156* off Nova Scotia and dynamited.

Friday ◑
22

565—Saint Columba reported seeing a monster in Loch Ness, Scotland.

Saturday
23

The gentleness of heaven is on the sea.
—William Wordsworth

Sunday
24

1927—The Nova Scotia Grand Banks schooner *Haligonian*, a competitor in the trials for the International Fishermen's Race trophy, was lost at sea with all hands.

YET AN OCEAN STEAMSHIP CAN STILL STIR THE PULSE

However much of actual beauty clings to a sail, and however much of traditional reverence bids us scorn an innovation, is there not something to be said for the grim, fire-spitting ocean steamer? In common with all steam devices the steamship has come in for a fair share of denunciation; but as a machine, as a resistless force, is there not something here to stir the pulses? As she sweeps down the harbour and over the bar, flags streaming, black smoke trailing, wide wake rolling, what could be finer!

—J. C. Van Dyke

SPECIFICATIONS OF THE *GREAT WESTERN*, THE LARGEST STEAMSHIP OF HER TIME

Length overall, figurehead to taffrail: 235 feet
Length between perpendiculars: 212 feet
Length of saloon: 75 feet
Tonnage: 1,320 tons
Best berths: 150
Crew berths: 26
Berths for engineers, firemen, and officers: 40
Power: 2 engines, 200 horsepower each
Bunkers: 600 tons of coal

"Good-bye, Romance!" the Skipper said;
"He vanished with the coal we burn;
Our dial marks full steam ahead,
Our speed is timed to half a turn.
Sure as the tidal trains we ply
'Twixt port and port. Romance, good-bye!"

—from "The King," by Rudyard Kipling

SHIPS THAT HAVE PASSED

A name on a printed page, an entry in some old log-book, sea-spotted and time-stained, in faded ink, and in the cramped, unaccustomed hand of one more used to handling tarry ropes than pens.... Ships that have passed—as the winds pass, as the waves pass—or as a bubble that, floating for a moment upon the face of the ever-moving waters, breaks into nothingness, and is gone....

—C. Fox Smith

THE TRANSATLANTIC STEAMSHIP *GREAT WESTERN*, AUGUST 30–31, 1844

August 30. Saw land to-day for the first time since we left Cape Clear; and heartily sick of the Atlantic. Saw Nantucket at two P.M. The atmosphere mild and warm. Paid my wine-bill to Crawford, the head steward. Finished my letters for England in hopes of catching the Boston steamer, which leaves New York at five P.M.

August 31. A beautiful morning. The wind changed. All the passengers on deck. The pilot (who had come out 160 miles to get the job, a very intelligent fellow) lent me a New York paper. A good many vessels in sight. Came close to Long Island. All bustle and confusion packing. Our boat did her best, but we saw we should be too late for the mail. Got to Sandy Hook at five; the Narrows at six; and up the East River at seven. Passed Fort Hamilton; and at half-past seven landed in New York. The confusion on landing baffled all description. Hundreds of pickpockets were on the look-out. We sojourned at the Astor House Hotel. Had a warm-bath, and retired to rest grateful that I was once more on Terra firma.

—George Moore

The wonders of the sea are as marvelous
as the glories of the heavens.
                    —Matthew Fontaine Maury

AUGUST

Monday
25 SUMMER BANK HOLIDAY / UK

1929—The raceboat *Imp* won the 1929 Gold Cup at
Red Bank, New Jersey.

Tuesday
26

1937—Charles W. Atwater arrived in Newport, Rhode
Island, in the cutter *Duckling* at the end of a passage
to Iceland and back; for this, he would receive the
Blue Water Medal of the Cruising Club of America.

Wednesday
27

1893—A hurricane struck the coast of South Carolina,
causing considerable damage to shipping and shore-
side structures and great loss of life.

Thursday
28

1609—Henry Hudson, exploring the east coast of North
America in the *Half Moon*, discovered Delaware Bay.

Friday ○
29

1782—The British warship *Royal George* sank suddenly at her moorings in Portsmouth Harbor, England,
while being careened for repairs below her waterline;
most of the crew was lost.

Saturday
30

INTERNATIONAL SEX BOMB DAY
(batten down the hatches)

Sunday
31

1910—Glenn Curtiss made the first airplane
flight over water, from Euclid Beach Park,
Cleveland, Ohio, to Cedar Point, Sandusky,
Ohio, a distance of 70 miles over Lake Erie.

THE U.S. GUNBOAT (FORMERLY YACHT) *GLOUCESTER*, OFF NEW YORK, SEPTEMBER 4, 1898

4 to 8 A.M. Course changed to north at 5.40, patent log 90.9. A sounding taken at six o'clock showed sixteen fathoms. Land sighted on port bow at 6.15 A.M. Made the Highlands at 6.45. Weather pleasant; numerous sails in sight. The Jersey shore in plain sight along the port side.

8 A.M. to noon. Clear and pleasant. Made Scotland lightship and ran in through Swash Channel. Made ship's name KJSV by international signal code to Sandy Hook station. Station signalled FDGS (welcome); replied DWQP (thanks). Many steamers saluted with whistles or cheered as we passed up the bay. Stopped a few minutes at Quarantine for pratique and went on to Tompkinsville. Exchanged numbers with *Indiana* and got permission to anchor. Anchored in six fathoms of water with thirty fathoms of chain. Ships of North Atlantic squadron at anchorage cheered as we steamed past.

—from the ship's log

FIRST NAMES, LAST NAMES, OTHER NAMES— A FEW DEFINITIONS

Bill—the end of an anchor's fluke, the part that bites into the ground

Bill of health—certificate indicating the state of health aboard a ship upon departure

Bill of lading—document listing the goods being transported aboard a ship

Bobstay—a stay leading from the end of the bowsprit to the stem at the cutwater

Davy Jones—the spirit of the sea

Davy Jones's locker—the bottom of the sea

Granny knot—an improperly tied reef or square knot

Guy—a line used to steady a spar

Handy Billy—a small tackle

Jack—another word for sailor; also a small flag

Jack in the basket—an old fishing term for a basket on a pole marking a shoal or the edge of a channel

Jack ladder—a ladder with side-rope handholds

Jack staff—a pole for flying the Union Jack

Jack-ass schooner—a schooner with one or more squaresails in addition to the foresail on the foremast

Jacob's ladder—a rope ladder with wooden treads

John Dory—a species of fish

Jolly Roger—the pirate's flag; black, decorated with a white skull and crossbones

Matthew Walker—a type of stopper knot

Mother Cary's chicken—sailors' name for the stormy petrel

Paddy's hurricane—dead calm

Peter boat—a small fishing boat formerly used on the River Thames, England

Roger's blast—a sudden squall

Stevedore—dockworker who loads and unloads ships

SAILING VESSEL TYPES IN THREE LANGUAGES

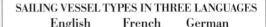

English	French	German
Full-rigged ship	Trois-mâts carré	Vollschiff
Bark	Barque	Bark
Brig	Brick	Brigg
Schooner	Goélette franche	Vor und hinter schooner
Sloop	Sloop	Slup
Cutter	Cotre	Kutter

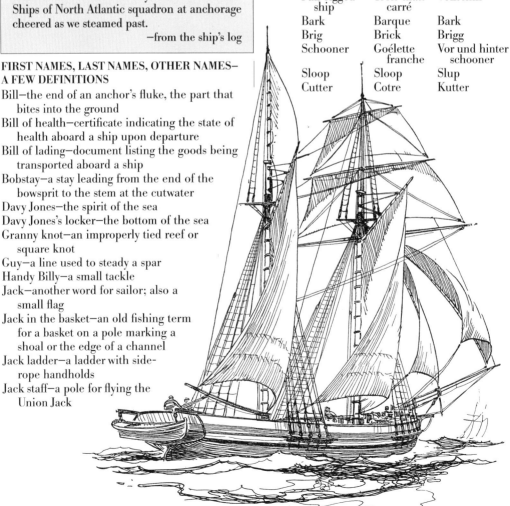

Yes! yes! give me this glorious ocean life,
this salt-sea life, this briny, foamy life.
    —from *Redburn*, by Herman Melville

SEPTEMBER

Monday

1
LABOR DAY / US & CANADA

1892—The steamer *Western Reserve* broke in two on Lake Superior and sank; 26 lives were lost.

Tuesday

2

1775—The armed schooner *Hannah*, commissioned by General George Washington, became the first vessel in the Continental Navy.

Wednesday

3

1929—The remains of a 234-foot houseboat belonging to the Roman emperor Caligula (first century AD) were exposed after the waters of Lake Nemi, 20 miles southeast of Rome, were drained by archaeologists.

Thursday

4

1810—Donald McKay, clipper-ship builder—notably, *Stag Hound, Flying Cloud, Great Republic,* and *James Baines*—was born in Shelburne County, Nova Scotia.

Friday ◐

5

1917—The *Viola*, the last wooden whaling ship to be built in the United States, set sail from New Bedford, Massachusetts, never to be heard from again.

Saturday

6

READ A BOOK DAY

Sunday

7

1952—The U.S. Coast Guard cutter *Courier*, anchored off the island of Rhodes, Greece, began broadcasting The Voice of America.

RULE, BRITANNIA

by James Thomson

When Britain first, at Heaven's
    command,
Arose from out the azure main,
This was the charter of her land,
And guardian angels sung this strain:
"Rule, Britannia, rule the waves;
Britons never will be slaves."

The nations, not so blest as thee
Must, in their turns, to tyrants fall;
While thou shalt flourish great and
    free,
The dread and envy of them all.
"Rule, Britannia, rule the waves;
Britons never will be slaves."

Still more majestic shalt thou rise,
More dreadful from each foreign stroke;
As the loud blast that tears the skies
Serves but to root thy native oak.
"Rule, Britannia, rule the waves;
Britons never will be slaves."

Thee haughty tyrants ne'er shall tame;
All their attempts to bend thee down
Will but arouse thy generous flame,
But work their woe, and thy renown.
"Rule, Britannia, rule the waves;
Britons never will be slaves."

To thee belongs the rural reign;
Thy cities shall with commerce shine;
All thine shall be the subject main;
And every shore it circles, thine.
"Rule, Britannia, rule the waves;
Britons never will be slaves."

The Muses, still with freedom found,
Shall to thy happy coast repair:
Blest isle! with matchless beauty
    crowned,
And manly hearts to guard the fair:
"Rule, Britannia, rule the waves;
Britons never will be slaves."

A NIGHT OF MUSIC

The night before the vessels were ready to sail, all the
Europeans united and had an entertainment at the Rosa's
hide-house, and we had songs of every nation and tongue.
A German gave us "Och! mein lieber Augustin!" the three
Frenchmen roared through the Marseilles Hymn; the
English and Scotchmen gave us "Rule Britannia," and
"Wha'll be King but Charlie?" the Italians and Spaniards
screamed through some national affairs, for which I was
none the wiser; and we three Yankees made an attempt at
the "Star-spangled Banner."
    —Richard Henry Dana Jr.

THE SCHOONER *LURLINE*, PACIFIC OCEAN OFF THE COAST OF CALIFORNIA, SEPTEMBER 10–11, 1919

Several land birds came aboard in the morning, and
not long afterward the brown slopes of Santa Rosa Island
took shape through the lifting fog. The heavens were
overcast all day, but for a brief space in the afternoon a
long strip of cloud ran back across the east like a sliding
door, and through the rift we had a brief glimpse of the
rugged Sierra Madres, a hundred miles distant, standing
sharp and distinct in a flood of sunshine against a vivid
background of California sky. Doing the best we could
with puffs of wind that came by turn from all points of
the compass, we crept along at three or four miles an
hour until midnight. Then it fell dead calm, and during
the next eight hours the log recorded but a single mile.
This was broken by a light westerly breeze and before
it, wing-and-wing, we went groping in through the fog,
watching for a landfall that would give us our position.
This appeared at noon, when the familiar cliffs of Point
Vicente began showing.
    —Lewis R. Freeman

SEPTEMBER

Monday
8

1997—The ferry *Pride of La Gonave* sank off Montrouis, Haiti; more than 200 lives were lost.

Tuesday
9

1934—The first Snipe class world championships were held; William E. Bracey of the Dallas Sailing Club took first place.

Wednesday
10

1889—The crews at the Lewes, Cape Henlopen, and Rehoboth Beach lifesaving stations, beginning on this day and continuing for three days, assisted 22 vessels and saved 194 people without the loss of a single life.

Thursday
11

1700—James Thomson, author of the lyrics to "Rule, Britannia," was born in Roxburgh, Scotland.

Friday
12

1922—The U.S. Shipping Board sold 233 surplus World War I merchant ships to the Western Marine and Salvage Company; cost to build, $300 million, price to buy, $750,000.

Saturday
13

2008—Olin J. Stephens II, yacht designer most famous for his 12-meter America's Cup defenders, passed away at age 100.

Sunday
14

1852—The clipper ship *Westward Ho!* was launched in East Boston, Massachusetts.

MAJOR OIL-TANKER DISASTERS

Torrey Canyon, March 8, 1967, off Cornwall, England, 38 million gallons of crude oil

Sea Star, December 1972, Gulf of Oman, 35 million gallons of crude oil

Argo Merchant, December 15, 1976, southeast of Nantucket Island, 7.7 million gallons of fuel oil

Hawaiian Patriot, February 1977, northern Pacific Ocean, 30 million gallons of oil

Amoco Cadiz, March 16, 1978, off Brittany, France, 68 million gallons of oil

Collision of *Atlantic Empress* and *Aegean Captain*, July 19, 1979, off Tobago, 46 million gallons of crude oil; later, while being towed, the *Atlantic Empress* spilled 41 million gallons off Barbados.

Castillo de Bellver, August 6, 1983, off Cape Town, South Africa, 250,000 tons of oil

Odyssey, November 10, 1988, near St. John's, Newfoundland, 43 million gallons of oil

Exxon Valdez, March 24, 1989, Prince William Sound, Alaska, 10 million gallons of oil

Kharg-5, December 19, 1989, north of Canary Islands, 19 million gallons of crude oil

Mega Borg, June 8, 1990, southeast of Galveston, Texas, 5.1 million gallons of oil

Haven, May 28, 1991, Genoa, Italy, 42 million gallons of oil

ABT Summer, May 28, 1991, off Angola, 15–78 million gallons of oil

Nagasaki Spirit, September 1992, Strait of Malacca, 12,000 tons of crude oil

Aegean Sea, December 1992, near La Coruña, Spain, 80,000 tons of oil

Braer, January 1993, Shetland Islands, 85,000 tons of crude oil

Sea Empress, February 15, 1996, Milford Haven, Wales, 70,000 tons of crude oil

Nakhodka, December 1997, Sea of Japan, 19,000 tons of oil

Erika, December 12, 1999, off Brittany, France, 3 million gallons of heavy oil

Westchester, November 28, 2000, Mississippi River near Port Sulphur, Louisiana, 567,000 gallons of crude oil

Prestige, November 2002, off coast of Spain, 20 million gallons of fuel oil

An officer, while in charge of the deck, should never allow his thoughts to wander from the subject of his immediate duties, to which end it would be well, during his earlier years, to adopt as an invariable rule the resolution never to think of anything but seamanship while actually on watch. —S. B. Luce, U.S. Navy

THE ARCTIC EXPLORATION SHIP *FRAM*, KARA SEA (NORTH OF SIBERIA), SEPTEMBER 20, 1893

As I was sitting at 11 A.M., looking at the map and thinking that my cup would soon be full—we had almost reached 78°—there was a sudden luff, and I rushed out. Ahead of us lay the edge of the ice, long and compact, shining through the fog. I had a strong inclination to go eastward, on the possibility of there being land in that direction but it looked as if the ice extended farther south there, and there was the probability of being able to reach a higher latitude if we kept west; so we headed that way. The sun broke through for a moment just now, so we took an observation, which showed us to be in about 77°44' north latitude. We now held northwest along the edge of the ice. It seemed to me as if there might be land at no great distance, we saw such a remarkable number of birds of various kinds. A flock of snipe or wading birds met us, followed us for a time, and then took their way south. They were probably on their passage from some land to the north of us. We could see nothing, as the fog lay persistently over the ice.   —Fridtjof Nansen

Monday
15

2001—The tug *Brown Water V* and four barges it was towing struck the Queen Isabella Causeway over the Intracoastal Waterway in Texas, causing a 240-foot section to collapse; 5 lives were lost.

Tuesday
16

1994—A federal jury ordered the Exxon Corporation to pay $5 billion in punitive damages to those harmed by the 1989 oil spill caused by the tanker *Exxon Valdez*, which went aground in Alaska.

Wednesday
17

1938—Malcolm Campbell, pushing *Bluebird* to a speed of 130.91 on Lake Hallwil, Switzerland, became the first driver of an unlimited speedboat to exceed 130 mph.

Thursday
18

1679—The brig *Le Griffon*, the first vessel built by Europeans on the Great Lakes, sank in a gale in Mackinaw Strait.

Friday
19

1846—A fierce gale struck the Grand Banks off Newfoundland, sinking 11 fishing schooners; 65 lives were lost.

Saturday
20

1519—Ferdinand Magellan got underway from Cadiz, Spain, with a squadron of 5 ships on a voyage of exploration that would lead to the first circumnavigation of the globe.

Sunday
21

1938—The Great Hurricane of '38, one of the most destructive on record, struck the northeast coast of the United States.

BEARS AT SEA

Bear away—ease the helm and the sheets so a vessel is sailing more or less before the wind

Bear down—go downwind toward an object

Bear off—an order to keep the vessel off an object

Bear a hand—appeal for assistance, quickly

ANIMAL SUPERSTITIONS

Bad luck

Getting underway with a pig or a rabbit on board

Seeing a cormorant or a curlew out of sight of land

Killing a porpoise

Saying the word *pig* out loud (rather, use the term *queer critter*)

Dreaming of a white horse at night (a gale will come the next day)

Rats leaving a leaking ship (the ship will sink)

A black cat that dies or is killed (the vessel will sink)

A cat that becomes frisky and fluffs its tail has "a gale in his tail" (strong winds are coming)

A swallow landing on a vessel (a storm is coming)

Stormy petrels (aka Mother Cary's chickens) nearby (a storm is coming)

Killing a stormy petrel or an albatross (the penalty is a life for a life)

Intentionally harming an albatross, or a spider, or a seagull (what you do to it will be done to you)

A shark following a ship (someone will die)

Counting the number of fish you have caught (you will catch no more)

Three seagulls directly overhead, flying together (death is near)

Good luck

Plenty of rats on board (the ship won't sink)

A cat on board

A dove out of sight of land

A rabbit's foot

The horn of a narwhal, or a unicorn

A shark-teeth necklace

Porpoises swimming around a ship

When the water reaches the upper level, follow the rats.
                              —Claude Swanson

THE SAILING SHIP *PACTOLUS*, SOUTH PACIFIC OCEAN WEST OF CHILE, SEPTEMBER 1879

September 22. During the morning, one of the sailors reported a boat drifting about to the eastward, and for a time there was quite a sensation on board, but at last the object turned out to be a number of large brown birds sitting on the water, and evidently feeding on something. Saw a great many nautiluses.

September 23. School of about a dozen right whales passed within one-quarter of a mile during the forenoon. This species blow a high straight stream, instead of the short puffs given by the sperm whales that we saw off Pernambuco, Brazil.

September 25. Second mate and one of the sailors indulged in a short row; one round fought, resulting in victory for the second mate.

                              —Morton MacMichael

SEPTEMBER

Monday
22

1968—The miniature yacht *Little One* was found in the Atlantic Ocean west of Ireland without her singlehanded skipper, William Willis; the log suggested the boat had been sailing herself for nearly three months.

Tuesday
23 AUTUMNAL EQUINOX

1853—The *North Star*, owned by Cornelius Vanderbilt, returned to New York, the first yacht to circumnavigate the globe.

Wednesday
24 FIRST DAY OF ROSH HASHANAH

The sea's most powerful spell is romance.
—H. W. Tilman

Thursday
25

1992—USS *Constitution*, the oldest ship in the U.S. Navy, went into drydock at the Old Navy Yard, Charlestown, Massachusetts, for a major restoration that would return her to sailing condition.

Friday
26

1899—The city of New York held a naval parade to welcome Admiral George Dewey, the victor in the Battle of Manila Bay during the Spanish-American War.

Saturday ○
27

1880—The ship *Chateaubriand*, caught in a typhoon in the South China Sea, recorded barometric readings that dropped from 29.64 to 27.04 inches in four hours.

Sunday
28

1827—The first night boat of the Fulton ferry line between Brooklyn and Manhattan, New York, commenced service.

THE BEAUFORT SCALE

Beaufort number	State of air	Velocity (in knots)
0	Calm	0–1
1	Light airs	1–3
2	Slight breeze	4–6
3	Gentle breeze	7–10
4	Moderate breeze	11–16
5	Fresh breeze	17–21
6	Strong breeze	22–27
7	Moderate gale	28–33
8	Fresh gale	34–40
9	Strong gale	41–47
10	Whole gale	48–55
11	Storm	56–65
12	Hurricane	above 65

BEAUFORT SCALE FOR YACHTS, SUGGESTED BY COMMANDER R. D. GRAHAM, R.N.

Beaufort number	State of air	Result
0	Calm	No steerageway
1	Light air	Just steerageway
2	Light breeze	Yachts handle comfortably and sail 2 to 3 knots.
3	Gentle breeze	Yachts sail 3 to 4 knots.
4	Moderate breeze	Yachts sail 4 to 5 knots with decided list and some motion; white tops appear on waves
5	Fresh breeze	Yachts sail at their maximum speed but are uncomfortable if close-hauled; topsails and light canvas taken in
6	Strong breeze	Yachts reef mainsails
7	High wind	Yachts close-reef, can just continue sailing to windward and make slight progress
8	Fresh gale	Yachts heave-to
9	Strong gale	Yachts lie "a-hull" or to a sea anchor
10	Whole gale	Yacht crews become desperate
11	Storm	
12	Hurricane	

HMS *PHOENIX*, CARIBBEAN SEA, OCTOBER 2, 1780

At eight o'clock a hurricane; the sea roaring, but the wind still steady to a point; did not ship a spoonful of water. However, got the hatchways all secured, expecting what would be the consequence, should the wind shift; placed the carpenters by the mainmast, with broad axes, knowing from experience that at the moment you may want to cut it away to save the ship, an axe may not be found. Went to supper; bread, cheese and porter. The purser frightened out of his wits about his bread bags; the two marine officers as white as sheets, not understanding the ship's working so much, and the noise of the lower deck guns; which by this time made a pretty screeching to people not used to it; it seemed as if the whole ship's side was going at each roll. Wooden, our carpenter, was all this time smoking his pipe and laughing at the Doctor; the Second Lieutenant upon deck, and the third in his hammock. At ten o'clock I thought to get a little sleep; came to look into my cot; it was full of water.

—one of her officers

f the Bermudas let you pass
You must beware of Hatteras.
                    —anon.

SEPT/OCT

Monday
29

1588—Queen Elizabeth I, while feasting on goose, learned of the defeat of the Spanish Armada; the tradition in England since then has been to eat goose on Michaelmas, the feast of St. Michael, which falls on this day.

Tuesday
30

1933—*El Lagarto* won the President's Cup on the Potomac River, Washington, DC, becoming the first big powerboat to win the National Sweepstakes, the Gold Cup, and the President's Cup in the same season.

Wednesday
1

1869—The Royal Hospital at Greenwich, England, a retirement home for seamen, was converted to an infirmary; it is now the site of Britain's National Maritime Museum.

Thursday
2

1931—Sir Thomas Johnstone Lipton, tea magnate (Lipton's Tea), multiple-time challenger for the America's Cup, died in London, England.

Friday
3 YOM KIPPUR

Two legendary U.S. aircraft carriers—*Lexington* (CV-2, 1925) and *Enterprise* (CV-6, 1936)—were launched on this day.

Saturday ◑
4

1976—Seven survivors of a Finnish motorboat that sank in the Baltic Sea were rescued by the USS *Jonas Ingram*.

Sunday
5

1893—The dynamite cruiser *Vesuvius* was ordered to destroy all floating derelicts along the Atlantic coast of the United States.

The matter of tasty and nourishing food when cruising is of the utmost importance. An underfed or poorly fed crew just won't be able to take the gaff, and there is no point in cruising if you can't take it.   —Eugene V. Connett III

The best victual of all is biscuit, because it needs neither to be ground, grated, salted, nor diluted and it keeps for over two years.
     —Georges Fournier, 17th century

THE SHANTYBOAT *EASY WAY*, ILLINOIS RIVER, MARCH 30, 1900

The Illinois here was not a wide stream, perhaps one hundred yards across. It was at a fair stage of water, so that the bank of the bottomland opposite, tree-covered and grassy, was but four or five feet above the water, and the intervening slope appeared from our side of the stream a grassy and inviting bank. On the right was the abrupt hillside of the two cities, La Salle and Peru, and, nearer, the stone revetment of the river bend. And in between was a ribbon of water without a flaw, with scarcely an eddy, without an audible murmur, with an appearance so peaceful, so trustworthy, so enticing, as to seem the natural habitat of honeymooners, given over entirely to thoughts not connected with the world about them.… In the cabin the tea-kettle sang noisily upon the stove. But on deck we two were the most peaceful, the most contented, the most relaxed objects in the whole scene.

     —John L. Mathews

BAKING POWDER BISCUITS

2 cups flour
4 teaspoonsful baking powder
1 teaspoonful salt
1 tablespoonful lard
1 tablespoonful butter
$^3/_4$ cup milk and water in equal parts

Mix the dry ingredients as well as you can with a spoon, then add the milk and water. Roll out and cut into biscuits, and bake about ten minutes in medium hot oven.

     —from *The ABC of Cooking, for Men with No Experience of Cooking on Small Boats*, 1917

MEAT SOUP, ENOUGH FOR THE ENTIRE CREW

16 $^1/_2$ lbs meat, 1 lb onions, 1 lb flour, 5 ozs salt, $^1/_2$ oz pepper, 5 ozs sugar, small faggot of herbs, and 3 $^1/_2$ gals water. Separate the large bone from the meat, also the gristle, cut the meat into pieces of about 4 ozs, take 8 ozs of the fat and chop it up, slice the onions, put the fat in the boiler; when melted, add the onions, stir them well, so that they do not get brown, in five minutes add the meat, which keep stirring and turning over for five minutes longer; the meat ought to be warm through. Then add the boiling water by degrees, let it simmer gently for an hour, mix the flour with cold water very smooth, add it to the soup with the salt, pepper, sugar, and herbs; simmer gently for thirty minutes, keep stirring it to prevent the flour from settling at the bottom. The great error commonly committed in making soup, is doing it too rapidly, which renders the meat hard and tasteless. Bones and scraps of meat should be collected after every meal and put down to simmer for next day's soup.

     —from *The Sailor's Pocket Book*, 1885

OCTOBER

Monday
5

962—The USS *Bainbridge*, the first nuclear-powered destroyer in the U.S. Navy, was commissioned.

Tuesday
7

1897—The Inland Rules of the Road became effective in U.S. waters.

Wednesday
8

BRING YOUR TEDDY BEAR TO WORK DAY

Thursday
9

1913—The sailing ship *Dalgonar*, after being knocked down during a storm in the Pacific Ocean, was abandoned; several months and approximately 5,000 miles later, she went aground on a reef off Maupihaa Island.

Friday
10

1818—The *Frontenac*, the first steamboat on the Great Lakes, got underway on her first voyage, from Buffalo, New York, to Detroit, Michigan.

Saturday
11

1896—The crew of the Pea Island Life-Saving Station saved all aboard the schooner *E.S. Newman*, aground on the North Carolina coast during a hurricane; they later received the Gold Lifesaving Medal.

Sunday
12

1914—The collier *Jupiter* became the first ship of the U.S. Navy to pass through the Panama Canal.

THE CRUISING YACHT *OENIADE*, COAST OF BRITTANY, FRANCE, OCTOBER 15, 1933

The topsail sets like a board now, so we hoisted it and sailed peacefully up the Chateaulin River to Le Folgoat Creek. Off Tibidy Island the tide turned against us and the wind failed, so we motored to our anchorage. The charming scenery of Terenez Island is marred by an ugly bunch of decaying French men-of-war, looking so shockingly out of place that they very nearly appear all right. We walked across the fine new suspension bridge before supper. It is a pitch dark, calm and utterly silent night. It is absolutely essential to lay out the kedge here. There is an excellent well of fresh water on the Northern side of the creek, above a lavoir, among the trees, about half way to the mill; easily approached at high water. Milk can be obtained from the Forester's cottage, above the Mill.

—M. L. Goldsmith

THERE ARE WAVES OF ALL SORTS, ACCORDING TO HILAIRE BELLOC

There was the Wave that brings good tidings, and the Wave that breaks on the shore, and the Wave of the island, and the Wave that helps, and the Wave that lifts forrard, the kindly Wave and the youngest Wave, and Amathea the Wave with bright hair, all the waves that come up round Thetis in her train when she rises from the side of the old man, her father, where he sits on his throne in the depth of the sea; when she comes up cleaving the water and appears to her sons in the upper world.

WAVE TERMINOLOGY

The length of a wave is the distance between successive crests or hollows.

The height of a wave is the vertical distance between crest and hollow.

The period of a wave is the time between the passage of successive crests past a fixed point.

WHEN WAVES BECOME DANGEROUS

A strong wind blows against, or at a sharp angle to, a preexisting swell.

A strong wind blows against a strong tide.

A shoal rises suddenly out of deep water.

The wind becomes so strong as to blow off the tops of the waves.

Waves are not measured in feet or inches, they are measured in increments of fear.
    —Buzzy Trent, big-wave surfer

I don't know who named them swells. There's nothing swell about them. They should have named them awfuls.
    —Hugo Vihlen

A smooth sea never made a skillful mariner.
—anon.

OCTOBER

Monday
13
THANKSGIVING / CANADA
COLUMBUS DAY / US

1907—The legendary tea clipper *Thermopylae*, having been renamed *Pedro Nunes* and converted to a coal barge, was towed to sea off the mouth of the Tagus River, Portugal, and sunk.

Tuesday
14

1947—The U.S. Coast Guard cutter *Bibb*, on ocean-station duty in the mid-Atlantic Ocean, rescued 62 passengers and 7 crew of the ditched transatlantic flying boat *Bermuda Sky Queen*.

Wednesday
15

1881—The inaugural issue of *American Angler*, the first monthly fishing magazine in the United States, was published in Philadelphia, Pennsylvania.

Thursday
16

1956—The SS *Mariposa*, the first ocean liner equipped with gyrostabilizers—specially designed fins to dampen rolling—was launched in Portland, Oregon.

Friday
17

There is a witchery in the sea, its songs and stories, and in the mere sight of a ship, and the sailor's dress.
—Richard Henry Dana Jr.

Saturday
18

1910—In the first ship–dirigible/sea–air rescue, the Royal Mail steamship *Trent* recovered the passengers and crew of the dirigible *America*, downed in the Atlantic Ocean.

Sunday
19

1844—A storm with hurricane-force southwesterly winds drove the waters of Lake Erie into downtown Buffalo, New York; approximately 200 lives were lost.

NATHANIEL HOLMES BISHOP, ADVENTURER

Adventuring, especially in small craft, became something of a craze on both sides of the Atlantic during the Victorian age, and one of its greatest exponents was Nathaniel Holmes Bishop (1837–1902). A believer in adventure for adventure's sake, he initially gained fame by hiking through South America when he was only 17 years old. His subsequent book, *The Pampas and Andes: A Thousand Miles' Walk Across South America*, published in 1869, became a bestseller. Five years later, influenced by the exploits of John MacGregor, an Englishman who popularized the decked double-paddle canoe, he cruised the inland waterways of North America from Quebec to the Gulf of Mexico. His boat

THE MISSION YACHT *ALLEN GARDINER*, BRISTOL, ENGLAND, OCTOBER 24, 1854

My little vessel was taken in tow by a steamer and proceeded down the river to King's Road. All the crew, artizans, catechist, and surgeon were on board; and every one of them, apparently, hopeful for the future. It was a rather dull, wet, and disagreeable morning, and something like a gloom hung on us, though sunshine might have been in the heart. Just before entering King's Road I thought it wise to receive a pledge from all on board that they would, severally and together, at all times, do their utmost towards carrying out the objects of the mission, and cordially support me in the arduous duties it would be my task to perform. I began with the crew, calling over each man's name, and asking whether he fully understood what he had come to do, and would sincerely act up to that which he had promised when signing the ship's agreement. The answer of all was in the affirmative.

—W. Parker Snow

of choice was an 18-foot wooden double-paddle canoe, but soon after departing he found the canoe to be too heavy for the many portages required. He gave it up for a canoe molded from heavy-duty paper and glue, a newly developed technique similar in theory to the fiberglass layup of today. He followed that adventure by taking a sneakbox, a type of duckboat, down the Ohio and Mississippi Rivers. His books, *Voyage of the Paper Canoe* (1878) and *Four Months in a Sneak-Box* (1879) are adventuring classics.

NATHANIEL HOLMES BISHOP III ESPIES THE PERFECT SMALL BOAT

To find such a boat—one that possessed many desirable points in a small hull—had been with me a study of years. I commenced to search for it in my boyhood.... I failed to discover the object of my desire, until, on the sea-shore of New Jersey, I saw for the first time what is known among gunners as the Barnegat Sneak-box.

*Man cannot discover new oceans unless he has
the courage to lose sight of the shore.*
—André Gide

OCTOBER

Monday ◑
20

1976—The Norwegian tanker *Frosta* collided with the
ferry *George Prince* on the Mississippi River near Luling,
Louisiana; 77 lives were lost.

Tuesday
21

1874—Nathaniel Holmes Bishop III began a voyage
from Troy, New York, to Cedar Key, Florida, in the *Maria
Theresa*, a canoe made of paper.

Wednesday
22

1921—The Lunenburg schooner *Bluenose* won the first
match of the second International Fishermen's Race,
defeating the Gloucester schooner *Elsie*.

Thursday
23

1988—The *Pride of Baltimore II*, a reproduction of a Baltimore clipper built to replace her namesake, which was lost
at sea in 1986, was commissioned in Baltimore, Maryland.

Friday
24

The entire ocean is affected by a pebble.
—Blaise Pascal

Saturday
25

1918—In one of the worst marine disasters on
the West Coast, the Canadian Pacific steamship
Princess Sophia was wrecked in the Lynn Canal,
Alaska, with the loss of 331 lives.

Sunday
26

1886—Birthday of Ralph E. Winslow, yacht designer
best known for powerboats and auxiliary sailboats.

THE STEAMBOAT *ALTON*, BELOW CAPE GIRARDEAU, MISSISSIPPI RIVER, OCTOBER 27, 1909

A cornfield slipping into the river was what the travelers saw as they came out from breakfast on the *Alton*. A wall of the richest soil in the world, twenty feet high, faced the river. On the surface the corn rows extended to the upper edge. At the bottom of the wall the water swirled and undermined. As the *Alton* passed, the chunks of land fell away and were swallowed with successive splashes. On the opposite side of the changing channel the sand bars stretched in square miles. The course of the river was a series of long, sweeping curves, now to the westward and then to the eastward. But the channel, the depth necessary for navigation, did not coincide with the curves of the banks. It zigzagged across the mile of water, first one way and then another.... The *Alton* headed to and fro across the river, almost at right angles, now toward a caving bank of one State and then toward a sand bar of the other State.

—Walter B. Stevens

Spar-makers in the spar-yard, the swarming row of well-grown apprentices,
The swing of their axes on the square-hew'd log, shaping it toward the shape of a mast,
The brisk short crackle of the steel driven slantingly into the pine,
The butter-color'd chips flying off in great flakes and slivers.... —Walt Whitman

WOODEN SPARS

The smaller the diameter of the spar, the clearer the timber required.

Best choice is Sitka spruce, white pine, or Douglas fir.

Spars should be finished bright so that developing rot will be visible (rot is difficult to detect in painted spars).

MOST LIKELY AREAS FOR ROT IN A WOODEN MAST

At the butt, where water can pool in the mast step

At the deck, where water can lodge between the mast wedges and the mast itself

At the spreaders, where water can collect where they are attached to the mast

In vertical checks, where water can run in and pool at the bottom.

MAST DIMENSIONS

Stick length (aka heel-to-truck)—height from one end to the other

Bury—depth from the top of the deck to the bottom of the mast step

Hounded length—from the top of the deck to the point where the shrouds are attached to the mast

Deck-to-pin—from the top of the deck to the sheave pin in the block for the main halyard

Wherein lies the lure of the sea?
—Rex Clemens

OCT/NOV

Monday ○
27

1869—The steamboat *Stonewall* caught fire and burned on the Mississippi River below Cairo, Illinois; approximately 200 lives were lost.

Tuesday
28

1892—The federal government transferred the steam sloop *Enterprise* to the Massachusetts Nautical Training School—the first maritime academy established by a state—for use as a training ship.

Wednesday
29

1911—Captain Klaus Larsen became the first person to successfully negotiate the Niagara River rapids in a motorboat, a 15-footer powered by an 8- to 10-hp, 2-cylinder Scripps engine.

Thursday
30

1808—Captain Benjamin Ireson of the schooner *Betty* was tarred, feathered, and run out of the town of Marblehead, Massachusetts, for not going to the aid of a vessel in distress.

Friday
31 HALLOWEEN

1941—More than a month before hostilities were declared between the United States and Germany, the USS *Reuben James*, on convoy duty, was sunk by the German submarine *U-562* in the Atlantic Ocean.

Saturday
1

1901—The keel was laid in Quincy, Massachusetts, for the seven-masted steel schooner *Thomas W. Lawson*, the only one of its type.

Sunday
2 DAYLIGHT SAVING TIME ENDS

1775—In one of the first naval appropriations, the Continental Congress earmarked $100,000 to carry out the responsibilities of the Marine Committee.

I have often heard seamen who have been used to ships all their lives declare that a 30-foot ship's launch would ride out a gale, when a yacht of 25 tons would be swamped.
—Tyrrel E. Biddle, 1883

THE CONFEDERATE STEAMER *SUMTER*, ISLAND OF MARTINIQUE, CARIBBEAN SEA, NOVEMBER 9, 1861

Weather fine during the morning. At daylight, got up steam and stood in for the land, running down the coast as we approached. The coast, all the way into the anchorage, is bold and clear. Ran within three hundred yards of Point Negro, passing a passenger steamer bound to St. Pierre, and anchored in six fathoms water, with the south end of the fort bearing E. 1/4 S., and the wharf about N. by E. A pilot soon after came on board, and we got under way, and went into the anchorage E. of the fort, the health officer visiting us in the meantime, and giving us pratique. Sent a lieutenant to call on the Governor, and afterwards visited him myself. I stated in this interview that I had came into Martinique to refresh my crew, and obtain such supplies as I needed, coal included. The Governor replied that he could not supply me with coal from the Government stock, but I was free to go into the market and purchase what I wanted.

—Captain R. Semmes, C.S.N.

If you want to understand the sea you've got to sail over it in a boat small enough to let you lean over the side and touch the Face of the Waters.
—Weston Martyr

THE PLEASURES OF SMALL CRAFT, ACCORDING TO R. D. "PETE" CULLER

Many folks nowadays say small craft don't offer a real challenge. To take some nice, classic small craft, with properly cut and sheeted sprit-sail, around some toy sand spit in what appear to be adverse conditions—there is a favorable eddy if you know where to find it and she works wonderfully in moderate going with only the tip of the board—takes as much experience as driving some hard-pressed schooner around some tide-ridden cape, and you don't get so wet!

SHIP'S BOATS, U.S. NAVY, LATE 19TH CENTURY

Launches, 28–34 feet
Steam cutters, 33 feet
First cutters, 26–30 feet
Second cutters, 24–28 feet
Third cutters, 24–28 feet
Fourth cutters, 26 feet
Whaleboats,
   27–29 feet
Barges, 30–32 feet
Gigs, 28–30 feet
Dinghies,
   18–20 feet

NOVEMBER

Monday ◑
3

1899—Jim Jeffries retained his heavyweight boxing title, defeating "Sailor Tom" Sharkey, a seaman with a schooner tattooed on his chest; Sharkey's motto was "Don't Give Up the Ship."

Tuesday
4

1875—The steamship *Pacific*, on a voyage between San Francisco, California, and Portland, Oregon, sank; 200 lives were lost.

Wednesday
5

1884—The *Henry B. Hyde*, one of the last sailing ships of the downeaster type, was launched in Bath, Maine.

Thursday
6

I dreamed a dream in sailor town, a foolish dream and vain,
Of ships and men departed, of old days come again.
—C. Fox Smith

Friday
7

1910—The five-masted bark *Preussen*, one of the largest sailing ships in the world, collided with a steamship in the English Channel and sank.

Saturday
8

1926—The *Governor Moore*, the first ferryboat in the United States built exclusively to carry cars, went into service between New York City and New Jersey on the Hudson River.

Sunday
9

1911—Howard Pyle, illustrator, author of *Howard Pyle's Book of Pirates* and *Tales of Pirates and Buccaneers*, died in Florence, Italy.

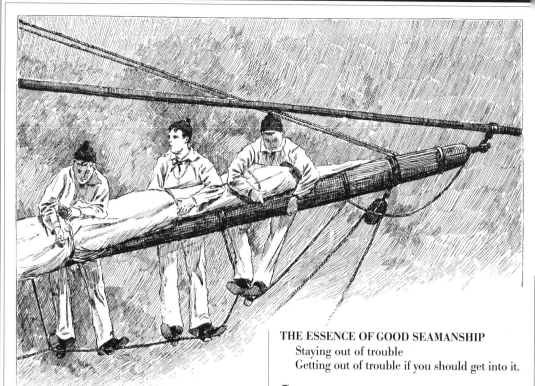

THE ESSENCE OF GOOD SEAMANSHIP
Staying out of trouble
Getting out of trouble if you should get into it.

Like fire, the sea is a good friend but a bad master, so you must never, never allow yourself to get into a position where the sea takes control.
—Uffa Fox

There is no royal road to the acquisition of seamanship. Experience is what is needed first, last and all the time. —Captain A. J. Kenealy

Seamanship may be described as an inexact science; it certainly cannot be reduced to a formula, nor learnt out of a book.
—Captain C. C. P. Fitzgerald

THE NOBLEST ART, ACCORDING TO THOMAS FLEMING DAY

I have been all my life a lover of the sea; an observer of its natural and social conditions; a student of its phases and fabrics; but while my mind in its long and wide search has touched upon almost every subject connected with ocean life, the one that has constantly interested and fascinated me is that which relates to the care and government of sailing vessels. This art, which is called seamanship, is one of man's oldest and noblest attainments.

KNOW YOUR VESSEL, SAYS CLAUD WORTH

The man who gets most enjoyment out of his sport, and who, if he desires it, can make long voyages in a small vessel in safety and comfort, is he who studies not only the sea and the seaman's art but who knows his own vessel intimately from keel to truck.

THE SCHOONER-YACHT *JOSEPHINE*, ATLANTIC OCEAN, NOVEMBER 13, 1874

A smooth sea, wind ahead, but light and refreshing. The morning is gorgeous, and it is pleasant to be moving along, although we are four points off our course. Decks are dry and available for exercise. The wretched wave-worn ducks and hens in their coop, forward, salute the sun with faint cackling, and quacking, as they absorb their matutinal corn, shedding a fragrance impossible to describe, and almost impossible to bear. At 12:30 P.M. we spoke the first vessel we have seen since leaving Sandy Hook, the barque *Volunteer*, bound for New York. She was lumbering along before the wind at a speed of about three knots an hour and it really was quite piratical, the saucy way in which our little schooner danced down to her, ran across her bows, tacked, and bore up under her stern, and we hailed her with a request to report us.
—W. P. Talboys

Monday
10

Look at the swoop of the eagle. The nearest we can approach to that is by a sail. —William Forwell

Tuesday
11
**REMEMBRANCE DAY / UK & CANADA
VETERANS DAY / US**

1897—The Gloucester fishing schooner *Helen G. Wells*, on Green Bank during a northwest gale, was knocked over until she was bottom up; a short while later, she righted herself and survived.

Wednesday
12

1925—The North American Yacht Racing Union, which had originally been founded in 1897 and expired a few years later, was reestablished.

Thursday
13

1851—A new submarine telegraph cable across the English Channel, to replace one that had failed, went into operation; as a test, a gun in Dover, England, was fired by remote control with a trigger in Calais, France.

Friday
14

1963—The tanker *Dynafuel* collided with the freighter *Fernview* in Buzzards Bay, capsized, and sank, causing a serious oil spill.

Saturday
15

1850—A contract was signed for the building of the schooner-yacht *America*: George Steers, designer; George Steers and W. H. Brown, builders.

Sunday
16

1841—A patent was issued to Napoleon E. Guerin of New York City for the first cork life preserver, a waistcoat containing pockets of granulated cork, "an improvement in buoyant dresses or life preservers."

When we sail with a freshening breeze,
  And landsmen all grow sick, sir,
The sailor lolls with his mind at ease.
  And the song and glass go quick, sir.
      Laughing here,
      Laughing there,
      Steadily, readily,
      Cheerily, merrily,
  Still from care and thinking free,
  Is a sailor's life at sea.

When the sky grows black and the winds blow
  hard,
  And landsmen skulk below, sir,
The sailor mounts to the topsail yard,
  And turns his quid as he goes, sir.
      Hauling here,
      Bawling there,
      Steadily, readily,
      Cheerily, merrily,
  Still from care and thinking free,
  Is a sailor's life at sea.

                          —from an old sea song

I have made up my mind now to be a sailor's
  wife,
To have a purse full of money and a very easy
  life,
For a clever sailor Husband is so seldom at his
  home,
That his Wife can spend the dollars with a will
  that's all her own,
Then I'll haste to wed a sailor, and send him
  off to sea,
For a life of independence is the pleasant life
  for me.
            —from "The Nantucket Girls Song," 1855

No man will be a sailor who has contrivance
enough to get him into a jail; for being in a
ship is being in a jail with the chance of being
drowned.
                          —Dr. Samuel Johnson

As we lay musing in our beds,
  So well and warm at ease,
I thought upon those lodging beds,
  Poor seamen have at seas.
                          —from an old sea song

HMS *BARFLEUR*, SOUDA BAY, CRETE, NOVEMBER 23, 1896

Manned and armed boats for quarterly firing. The three Cutters and the Launch and Pinnace were sent away in tow of the Steam Pinnace and Picket Boat. The wind being favourable, the boats in tow set sail. On arriving at a point three miles outside the Entrance to the Bay, the Boats cast off the tow and formed single line abreast, firing at a mark to expend quarterly allowance of ammunition. On completing the practice the boats returned independently as the Picket Boat had to take the Steam Pinnace, whose engines had broken down, in tow. The Picket Boat's Anchor was slung on the Towing Hawser to reduce the jerking strains due to the following sea running. Unarmed boats. German Frigate *Molkte* arrived and anchored. She is a full rigged ship and is utilized as a training ship. The heel of her Jibboom is not secured on the Bowsprit with a crupper band, but extends right inboard, as is the case in most Russian ships. This is due to the shortness of the Bowsprits which are built into these ships.

                          —from a midshipman's log

Monday
17

1973—The U.S. Coast Guard cutter *Polar Sea*, the largest icebreaker to date in the Western world, was launched.

Tuesday
18

1903—A treaty between Panama and the United States ceded to the United States in perpetuity "the use, occupation, and control of the zone of land and land under water, for the construction…of [a] canal."

Wednesday
19

1861—The brig *Elizabeth Watts* got underway from Philadelphia on a voyage to London, England, with the first shipment of petroleum, in barrels, from the United States to Europe.

Thursday
20

1620—Peregrine White, son of William and Susanna White, the first child born of English parents in present-day New England, was born aboard the Pilgrim ship *Mayflower* in Massachusetts Bay.

Friday
21

1922—The *Laconia* of the Cunard Line got underway from New York City on the first circumnavigation of the globe by a cruise ship; she returned on March 30, 1923.

Saturday
22

1906—The wireless signal "SOS" was adopted by the International Radio Telegraphic Convention as the official signal for distress at sea.

Sunday
23

1908—Murray G. Peterson, yacht designer, was born in Cape Elizabeth, Maine.

*They went to sea in a Sieve, they did,
   In a Sieve they went to sea:
In spite of all their friends could say,
On a winter's morn, on a stormy day,
   In a Sieve they went to sea!
And when the Sieve turned round and
   round,
And everyone cried, "You'll all be
   drowned!"
They cried aloud, "Our Sieve ain't big,
But we don't care a button, we don't
   care a fig!
   In a Sieve we'll go to sea!"*
   —from "The Jumblies," by Edward Lear

COURAGE IS THE KEY TO SAFETY, ACCORDING TO CARL LANE

Experience, knowledge, judgment, sense, and courage—and of these courage is probably the greatest. It takes courage to remain in port when the barometer predicts a storm beyond the pleasant sky. It takes courage to abandon a sail because of some minor failure of gear. It takes courage to refuse to make a night run because of lack of navigational skill. But boats skippered like that do not get into trouble very often.

THE POLAR EXPLORATION SHIP *BELGICA*, EASTERN ENTRANCE TO THE STRAIT OF MAGELLAN, NOVEMBER 29, 1898

At noon we rounded the low sandy bar extending southward from Cape Virgins terminating in Dungeness Point, and entered the historic Strait of Magellan. The eastern beach was strewn with fragments of iron from the hull of the iron vessel *Cleopatra*, which was one of the many vessels wrecked here. The skeleton of the *Cleopatra* was still fighting the sea some distance off shore, and presented a picture which would run into delight under the brush of an artist. The western shore of the point was strewn with fragments of wooden vessels, and two hulls well ashore rocked like cradles, but were apparently not much injured. This point seems to be a convenient graveyard for marine crafts.... The waters were alive with innumerable forms of life, many of which were new to us. Whales, seals, porpoises and penguins were darting about in the sea like birds in the air, while resting on the glassy surface, hovering over the land, rushing over and around the *Belgica* were strange members of the feathered tribe; among these, albatrosses, gulls, petrels, ducks, and geese were most numerous.
                              —Frederick A. Cook

U.S. COAST GUARD SAFETY REGULATIONS FOR PLEASURE BOATS COVER THE FOLLOWING AREAS

   Personal flotation devices
   Fire extinguishers —portable and fixed
   Engine-room ventilation
   Sound signaling devices—whistles and bells
   Inboard engine backfire flame arresters
   Visual distress signals
   Navigation lights

The regulations vary according to the size of the boat. For specific information on your requirements, contact the nearest Coast Guard station, or go to www.uscg.mil.

Prevention is, as in other aspects of seamanship, better than cure.
—Sir Robin Knox-Johnston

NOVEMBER

Monday
24

1815—Birthday of Grace Darling, who, with her father William, a lightkeeper on the Farne Islands, Northumberland, gained fame for the daring rescue of survivors from a shipwreck.

Tuesday ○
25

1837—Captain Thomas H. Sumner, in the Irish Sea, took a sun sight through the clouds and from it developed a technique of navigation since known as Sumner's Line.

Wednesday
26

1817—George Crowninshield, owner of *Cleopatra's Barge*, considered to be the first American offshore cruising yacht, died in Salem, Massachusetts.

Thursday
27

1926—The knockabout *Helen B. Thomas*, the first Gloucester fishing schooner rigged without a bowsprit, was destroyed by fire while serving as a Bermuda pilot boat.

Friday
28 THANKSGIVING / US

1720—Anne Bonney and Mary Read were convicted of piracy.

Saturday
29

1890—The U.S. Naval Academy defeated the U.S. Military Academy 24–0 in the first Army–Navy football game.

Sunday
30

1901—The ferryboats *Sausalito* and *San Rafael* collided in heavy fog in San Francisco Bay, sinking the *San Rafael*; 3 lives were lost, but more than 700 passengers were saved.

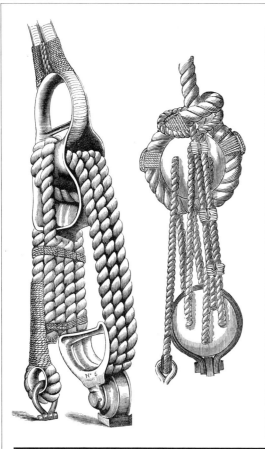

LIGHT CORDAGE IN THE AGE OF SAIL

"Small stuff"—the generic term for all light cordage, identified by the number of threads it contained ("18-thread stuff," "15-thread stuff") or by a specific name ("seizing stuff," "ratline stuff," "marline," "spun-yarn")

Spun-yarn—rough, cheap stuff, loosely laid up, left-hand lay, of two, three, or four strands; used for seizings and service where neatness wasn't required

Marline (two-strand, left-hand lay), houseline (three-strand, left-hand lay), roundline (three-strand, right-hand lay)—all superior to spun-yarn in quality; used for seizings and service when neatness was required

Seizing-stuff—used for seizings and service where high strength and extreme neatness were required. It was made by ropemaking machinery and was three-strand, right-hand lay, with two, three, or four threads to the strand. The greater the number of threads, the higher the quality of the stuff.

Ratline-stuff—similar to seizing-stuff, but larger; three-strand, right-hand lay, with four, five, six, seven, and even eight threads to the strand

Rope-yarns—remnants of old cordage, untwisted and tarred; used for temporary seizings and other quick, temporary work

Foxes—two rope-yarns twisted together by hand, or single yarns twisted against their natural lay, and rubbed smooth; used for light seizings

NATURAL FIBERS USED IN ROPEMAKING

Manila	Hemp	Jute	Cotton
Sisal	Coir	Flax	

SYNTHETIC FIBERS USED IN ROPEMAKING

Nylon
Polyester (Dacron)
Polypropylene
Kevlar

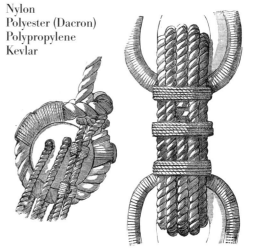

THE SAILING SHIP *SESOSTRIS*, ATLANTIC OCEAN AT THE EQUATOR, DECEMBER 5, 1829

Altogether a pleasant day till towards the evening when a quarel ensued the commencement of it was this Charles Grant A.B. was sitting on the forehatches singing. The Capt sent Mr Dresser Midshipman forward to tell him if he could not sing a better song then that to hold his tongue; he told him to tell the Capt that he would not hold his tongue, with that the Capt came forward and told him if he did not do as he had ordered him he would flog him, he told the Capt that he would not, the Capt and Grant stood talking for some time and the Capt colered him and with the help of two mates got him aft to put him in irons when a scufle ensued and E. Davis went and struck the Capt and told him he was going to bounce him. Immediately J. Hamilton and J. Anderson Baker interfeared and they were all put in irons but were soon released on acct of the rest of the Ships Comp leaving their duty but they told the Capt that they did not want to be released.

—James Smith

DECEMBER

Monday
1

1914–The first training school for naval aviators in the United States, the Navy Aeronautic Station, opened in Pensacola, Florida.

Tuesday
2

1821–George Washington Sears ("Nessmuk"), woodsman, author, and champion of ultralight canoes, was born in Oxford Plains, Massachusetts.

Wednesday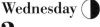
3

1787–A steamboat propelled by a stream of water forced out by a steam-powered pump, designed and built by James Rumsey, was demonstrated on the Potomac River near Shepherdstown, West Virginia.

Thursday
4

1843–Manila paper, made from recycled canvas sails and old rope, was patented.

Friday
5

PLAY HOOKY DAY
(and why not?)

Saturday
6

1988–The Swedish warship *Vasa*, sunk in 1628 and raised intact in 1961, was moved to a new museum specially built for her in Stockholm, Sweden.

Sunday
7

Two U.S. battleships–*New Jersey* (1942) and *Wisconsin* (1943)–were launched on this day.

ITEMS TO BRING ALONG WHEN TAKING TO
THE BOATS IN THE EVENT OF A SHIP'S SINK-
ING, A LIST FROM THE LATE 19TH CENTURY

Captain—compass, Maury on Navigation,
sextant, spy glass, Nautical Almanac, pencils and
writing paper, general chart, pocket watch, pair
of compasses, etc.

First mate—oars, masts, sails, boat-hooks,
bolts of canvas, boat's compass, Bowditch's chart,
ensign

Second mate—two or three bags of biscuits,
some breakers of water, quadrant, pencils and
writing paper, half-gill measure, a musket, box
of cartridges, and flints or caps

Surgeon—pocket instruments

Carpenter—hammer, nails, sheet-lead, grease,
oakum, saw, chisel, turn-screw, cold chisel, a vial
of sweet oil, any small iron rod

Third mate, or boatswain—coil of inch rope,
long reel, deep-sea reel, painted canvas, mar-
ling-spikes, spun-yarn, etc.

Sail maker—palm, needles, twine, fish-
ing-lines, hooks, painted canvas, boat's awning

Cook, and steward—tinder-box, flints and
tinder, small box, lantern and candles, cheese,
cabin biscuit, chocolate

Each person—a tin pot, a pocket knife, a
change of flannels and stockings

THE MARINER
by Robert Southey

O God! have mercy in this dreadful hour
On the poor mariner! in comfort here
Safe sheltered as I am, I almost fear
The blast that rages with resistless power.
What were it now to toss upon the waves,
The madden'd waves, and know no succour
   near;
The howling of the storm alone to hear,
And the wild sea that to the tempest raves;
To gaze amid the horrors of the night
And only see the billow's gleaming light;
Then in the dread of death to think of her
Who, as she listens sleepless to the gale,
Puts up a silent prayer and waxes pale?
O God! have mercy on the mariner!

THE SCHOONER-YACHT *NYANZA*,
AMONG THE FALKLAND ISLANDS, SOUTH
ATLANTIC OCEAN, DECEMBER 8, 1887

We were under way at 5 A.M., in tow of the
Swallow, bound for Speedwell Island, another
of the group. On our way we passed the *Star of
Scotia*, a barque which had been wrecked about
three months previously. All her masts and spars
were standing, and she looked as if she had really
sustained no damage. The rocks were, however, I
was told, sticking up through her keel. The crew
deserted her when she struck, and went off in two
boats. That commanded by the captain reached
the shore in safety, but the one in charge of the
mate was capsized, every man in her being
drowned. She was laden with wheat, and after
the wreck, was bought by Williams, of Stanley,
for £25.
          —J. Cumming Dewar

Monday
8

1875—The Committee of Lloyd's Register published the first load-line marking specifications for commercial vessels.

Tuesday
9

2000—The yacht *Union Bancaire Privée* set a record to date for the longest distance run in 24 hours by a singlehanded monohull, 430.7 nautical miles, in the Southern Ocean.

Wednesday
10

1907—Rudyard Kipling, author of *Captains Courageous*, was awarded the Nobel Prize for literature.

Thursday ●
11

Sailors, with their built-in sense of order, service and discipline, should really be running the world.   —Nicholas Monsarrat

Friday
12

1914—Richard Patrick Russ, better known as Patrick O'Brian, author of the Aubrey–Maturin series of historical naval novels, was born in Buckinghamshire, England.

Saturday
13

1693—Willem van de Velde the Elder, Dutch marine painter, died in Amsterdam.

Sunday
14

1938—The *Theresa E. Connor*, the last salt bank schooner to sail out of Lunenburg, Nova Scotia, and currently the centerpiece of the Fisheries Museum of the Atlantic, was launched in Lunenburg.

SHIP'S BELLS

The ship's clock strikes in a half-hour sequence based on the
    four-hour ship's watch system.
The end of the first half hour is marked by 1 bell
The end of the first hour is 2 bells
The end of the first 1 1/2 hours is 3 bells, etc.
The end of a four-hour watch is marked by 8 bells.
Eight bells are struck six times in a 24-hour period: at 12
    noon, 4 p.m., 8 p.m., 12 midnight, 4 a.m., and 8 a.m.

NOTICE POSTED IN THE *BOSTON* (MASSACHUSETTS) *GAZETTE*, DECEMBER 16, 1776

To be sold at Public Auction, the prize brig *Betsey*, about
120 tons burthen; an English built vessel, well found, with
sails and rigging; her cables about 100 fathom, each almost
new, with a hawser pretty wore, 3 good anchors, boat, &c.
Inventory to be seen, and vessel and appurtenances to be
reviewed any time before the sale, by applying to Benjamin
Burdick, Auctioneer. At the same Time and Place, Will be
Sold at Vendue, A Fine English cable, call'd 130 fathom in
length, full 12 inches, about 3800 wt.;never used; 2 hawsers
of 5 inch, about 100 fathom each, partly worn; 1 anchor of
800 wt; 1 ditto of 200 wt. 4 new short cannon, 2 pounders; 4
new swivels, well mounted; 2 fine copper stoves, with all the
apparatus; a new foresail, main-sail and top-sail, of the best
English duck, fit for a brig of 180 to 200 tons; several other
very good brig's sails; a sloop's jibb almost new; a chest of
carpenter's tools, consisting of saws, auger, caulking irons,
axes, hammers, mawls, cannippers, plane, &c. &c. 2 brass
compasses.

STRIKE THE BELL

an old pumping chanty

Aft on the poopdeck,
    Walking about,
There is the second mate,
    So sturdy and so stout;
What he is thinking of,
    He only knows himself,
Oh, we wish that he would hurry
up,
    And strike, strike the bell.

Strike the bell, second mate,
    Let us go below,
Look away to windward,
    You can see it's going to blow;
Look at the glass,
    You can see that it is fell,
We wish you would hurry up,
    And strike, strike the bell.

Down on the maindeck,
    Working at the pumps,
There is the larboard watch,
    Ready for their bunks;
Over to windward,
    They see a great swell,
They're wishing that the second
mate,
    Would strike, strike the bell.

Aft at the wheel,
    Poor Anderson stands,
Grasping the spokes,
    In his cold, mittened hands;
Looking at the compass,
    The course is clear as hell,
He's wishing that the second mate,
    Would strike, strike the bell.

For'ad in the fo'c'sle head,
    Keeping sharp lookout,
There is Johnny standing,
    Ready for to shout;
"Lights burning bright, sir,
    And everything is well,"
He's wishing that the second mate,
    Would strike, strike the bell.

Aft on the quarterdeck,
    The gallant captain stands,
Looking to windward,
    With his glasses in his hand;
What he is thinking of,
    We know very well,
He's thinking more of shortening
sail,
    Than strike, strike the bell.

A ship is a bit of terra firma cut off from the main; it is a state in itself; and the captain is its king.
—Herman Melville

DECEMBER

Monday
15

1839—A great gale struck the New England coast; 30 fishing schooners in Gloucester, Massachusetts, were dismasted and 20 went ashore.

Tuesday
16 FIRST DAY OF HANUKKAH

1497—Vasco da Gama rounded the Cape of Good Hope, the first European to do so.

Wednesday
17

1927—The submarine *S-4*, barely submerged, running underwater trials in Provincetown Harbor, Cape Cod, was run down and sunk by the U.S. Coast Guard cutter *Paulding*; there were no survivors.

Thursday
18

1865—The Navy Department ordered that the *United States*, built in 1797, one of the first six frigates in the U.S. Navy, be broken up.

Friday
19

1866—Eight men were washed overboard from the yacht *Fleetwing*, which was competing in the Great Ocean Race from New York to Cowes, England; two men were recovered, six were lost.

Saturday
20

1939—The ashes of Felix Riesenberg, deepwater sailor and author of *Under Sail, Cape Horn*, and other works, were scattered at sea off New York.

Sunday
21 WINTER SOLSTICE

1850—The extreme clipper ship *Witchcraft*, designed by Samuel Pook and built by Paul Curtis, was launched in Chelsea, Massachusetts.

*At evening off some reedy
    bay
You will swing slowly on your
    chain,
And catch the scent of dewey
    hay,
Soft blowing from the pleas-
    ant plain.*
    —from "Off Rivière du Loup,"
        by Duncan Campbell Scott

A FEW DON'TS WHEN BEACHING A BOAT

Don't beach the boat on a rising tide, otherwise the hull will be susceptible to pounding.

Don't beach the boat at the highest point of a high tide, as the next tide might not rise as high.

Don't beach the boat where a heavy swell is running, or she'll pound.

THE YAWL *BLUE DRAGON*, AMONG THE INNER HEBRIDES, SCOTLAND, DECEMBER 25, 1901

On Christmas morning the skipper and the Q.M. bathed and found the water quite warm, though the boy and the 2nd were incredulous and funked it. After breakfast we set off for Castle Gylen, a delightful old ruin built by the Macdougall of Lorne, dating back to the 13th century. The skipper sketched, while the crew explored the castle, taking photos and inspecting the geological peculiarities which had been pointed out to them. Then we hurried back to our Christmas dinner of turkey and plum-pudding, and blessed the providence of the skipper, though the 2nd protested that the A. and N. plum-pudding could be bought for half price at Oxford. The 2nd has a great turn for economy, but he couldn't deny the excellence of the dinner. In the afternoon we…sailed for Oban to fill up deficiencies in our stores, and to get young Nebby, the new oil-stove, who showed signs of being objectionable, into working order. We got all we required on board by dark and sailed back in the moonlight to the Little Horse Shoe. On our arrival the skipper spent hours in lining with felt the bunks of the 2nd and boy, which he did with great skill and toil, and with good results. The bunks were now all warm and quite watertight.

—C. C. Lynam

ANCHORING A DINGHY OR ROWBOAT OFF SHORE

Balance the anchor on the bow of the boat.

Coil the anchor line in the bottom of the boat so it will run out freely.

Make fast a tripline to the crown of the anchor.

While standing on the shore, coil the tripline at your feet so it will run out freely. Make sure the bitter end is secure.

Push the boat away from the shore.

When the boat reaches the proper spot, give the tripline a sharp jerk to pull the anchor overboard.

Make fast the tripline to a tree or rock on the shore.

To retrieve the boat, pull in the anchor by the tripline.

NOTE: This method only works if the tripline is made ast to the crown of the anchor! The best type of anchor for this is a grapnel.

Out of sight of land the sailor feels safe. It is the beach that worries him.
—Charles G. Davis

Monday
22

1938—A coelocanth, a fish thought to have become extinct 70 million years ago, was caught off Chalumna Point, South Africa.

Tuesday
23

1787—HMS *Bounty*, Lt. William Bligh in command, set sail from Portsmouth, England, for Tahiti to load a cargo of breadfruit trees.

Wednesday
24 CHRISTMAS EVE

1980—The U.S. Congress passed the Inland Navigational Rules Act, which superseded the old Inland, Western Rivers, and Great Lakes Rules.

Thursday ○
25 CHRISTMAS DAY

1492—Christopher Columbus's caravel *Santa Maria* was wrecked in the West Indies off what is now the Dominican Republic.

Friday
26 FIRST DAY OF KWANZAA
BOXING DAY / UK & CANADA

1853—The clipper ship *Great Republic*, the largest wooden ship built in America, yet to make her maiden voyage, burned to the waterline in New York City; she was later reconstructed.

Saturday
27

1853—The clipper ship *Comet* departed San Francisco on what would become a record passage for commercial sailing vessels of 76 days, 7 hours, to New York.

Sunday
28

With all its vicissitudes I still love a life on the broad, free ocean, never regretting the choice of my profession.
—Captain Joshua Slocum

THE U.S. FRIGATE *CONSTELLATION*,
PROPOSED DESIGN FOR HER FIGUREHEAD, DECEMBER 31, 1798

NATURE is crested with fire, her waist is encircled with the zone or signs of the zodiac, her hair and drapery loose and flowing, her right arm and head elevated, her left arm lightly resting on a large sphere, on which the Constellation is rising, her feet on a rock, part of which is formed into a rude pyramid, allegorical of the rapid and natural Union of the States, which took place at the commencement of the revolution, and supports the sphere aforementioned.

The Flame ascending from the top of the rock, is expressive of the fire which gave energy to the Patriots; the Water descending from the rock is an allusion to that Temperance peculiarly characteristic of the American revolution; the Scale and Mirror, at the foundation of the Pyramid, emblematic of the Truth and Justice of the cause: the Figure of the Dove or bird of peace, resting in the cap of Liberty expressive of Peace & Freedom, as principal objects of the revolution; the Herculean club encircled with laurel, is emblematic of that heroic Virtue that defended and obtained the cause; the Broad rock on which the figure stands, is emblematic of that Independence which was the Ultimate end of the Revolution. The Seasons represented in the trail crowning the Muses, as a pledge of the Free and Uninterrupted progress in all the pleasing branches of Science that open to View in the new World.

The sails are furled, our work is done,
Leave her, Johnny, leave her,
And now ashore we'll have some fun;
It's time for us to leave her. —from an old chanty

Monday
29

1812–The USS *Constitution*, under the command of Captain William Bainbridge, defeated HMS *Java* off the coast of Brazil.

Tuesday
30

1977–The U.S. Coast Guard's ocean station program came to an end when the cutter *Taney* departed Ocean Station Hotel and was replaced by a buoy.

Wednesday
31 NEW YEAR'S EVE

1600–The English East India Company, one of the greatest maritime trading companies of its time, was founded.

Thursday
1 NEW YEAR'S DAY

1920–The International Rule introduced by the International Yacht Racing Union in 1908 was revised; among other changes, centerboards were prohibited.

Friday ◐
2

"BOOGIE WOOGIE BUGLE BOY" DAY
(recorded by the Andrews Sisters, 1941)

Saturday
3

1912–Rear Admiral Robley D. Evans, USN, hero of the Spanish-American War and veteran of the round-the-world cruise of the Great White Fleet, died in Washington, DC.

Sunday
4

2013–Fred Brooks –clam digger, raconteur, bon vivant, part owner and longtime skipper of *Bugsy's Boomer*–shouldered an oar, walked inland until someone asked him what that thing was he was carrying, and retired on the spot.

2014

January

S	M	T	W	T	F	S
			1	2	3	4
5	6	7	8	9	10	11
12	13	14	15	16	17	18
19	20	21	22	23	24	25
26	27	28	29	30	31	

February

S	M	T	W	T	F	S
						1
2	3	4	5	6	7	8
9	10	11	12	13	14	15
16	17	18	19	20	21	22
23	24	25	26	27	28	

March

S	M	T	W	T	F	S
						1
2	3	4	5	6	7	8
9	10	11	12	13	14	15
16	17	18	19	20	21	22
23	24	25	26	27	28	29
30	31					

April

S	M	T	W	T	F	S
		1	2	3	4	5
6	7	8	9	10	11	12
13	14	15	16	17	18	19
20	21	22	23	24	25	26
27	28	29	30			

May

S	M	T	W	T	F	S
				1	2	3
4	5	6	7	8	9	10
11	12	13	14	15	16	17
18	19	20	21	22	23	24
25	26	27	28	29	30	31

June

S	M	T	W	T	F	S
1	2	3	4	5	6	7
8	9	10	11	12	13	14
15	16	17	18	19	20	21
22	23	24	25	26	27	28
29	30					

July

S	M	T	W	T	F	S
		1	2	3	4	5
6	7	8	9	10	11	12
13	14	15	16	17	18	19
20	21	22	23	24	25	26
27	28	29	30	31		

August

S	M	T	W	T	F	S
					1	2
3	4	5	6	7	8	9
10	11	12	13	14	15	16
17	18	19	20	21	22	23
24	25	26	27	28	29	30
31						

September

S	M	T	W	T	F	S
	1	2	3	4	5	6
7	8	9	10	11	12	13
14	15	16	17	18	19	20
21	22	23	24	25	26	27
28	29	30				

October

S	M	T	W	T	F	S
			1	2	3	4
5	6	7	8	9	10	11
12	13	14	15	16	17	18
19	20	21	22	23	24	25
26	27	28	29	30	31	

November

S	M	T	W	T	F	S
						1
2	3	4	5	6	7	8
9	10	11	12	13	14	15
16	17	18	19	20	21	22
23	24	25	26	27	28	29
30						

December

S	M	T	W	T	F	S
	1	2	3	4	5	6
7	8	9	10	11	12	13
14	15	16	17	18	19	20
21	22	23	24	25	26	27
28	29	30	31			